Skills Practice

for

Algebra I

Third Edition

Expressions, Equations, and Applications

by

Paul A. Foerster

Prepared by Isobel Zsohar

Addison-Wesley Publishing Company
Menlo Park, California • Reading, Massachusetts • New York
Don Mills, Ontario • Wokingham, England • Amsterdam • Bonn
Paris • Milan • Madrid • Sydney • Singapore • Tokyo
Seoul • Taipei • Mexico City • San Juan

ISBN 0-201-86098-8

4 5 6 7 8 9 10 -ML- 99 98

Contents

SKILLS PRACTICE 1
Review of Fractions

Use the Greatest Common Factor to write in lowest terms.

1. $\dfrac{6}{8}$ _____ **2.** $\dfrac{12}{28}$ _____

3. $\dfrac{20}{75}$ _____ **4.** $\dfrac{48}{32}$ _____

Find the common denominator by stating the Least Common Multiple.

5. $\dfrac{5}{12}, \dfrac{7}{8}$ _____ **6.** $\dfrac{5}{16}, \dfrac{9}{24}$ _____

7. $\dfrac{3}{14}, \dfrac{9}{35}$ _____ **8.** $\dfrac{7}{20}, \dfrac{9}{10}$ _____

Write the mixed numbers as improper fractions.

9. $8\dfrac{3}{4}$ _____ **10.** $12\dfrac{5}{6}$ _____

Change the improper fractions into mixed numbers.

11. $\dfrac{23}{15}$ _____ **12.** $\dfrac{12}{8}$ _____

Perform the indicated operations. Write all answers in lowest terms. If the result is improper, write it as the equivalent mixed number.

13. $\dfrac{2}{3} + \dfrac{4}{3}$ _____ **14.** $\dfrac{5}{6} - \dfrac{1}{6}$ _____

15. $\dfrac{3}{4} - \dfrac{2}{3}$ _____ **16.** $7\dfrac{1}{2} + 8\dfrac{3}{4}$ _____

Multiply the given fractions and write in lowest terms.

17. $\dfrac{3}{4} \times \dfrac{5}{6}$ _____ **18.** $\dfrac{7}{8} \times \dfrac{6}{5}$ _____

Multiply the mixed numbers after changing to equivalent improper fractions. Write in lowest terms.

19. $4\dfrac{1}{2} \times 3\dfrac{1}{2}$ _____ **20.** $5\dfrac{2}{3} \times 8$ _____

Write the reciprocal.

21. $\dfrac{3}{4}$ _____ **22.** $2\dfrac{1}{2}$ _____ **23.** $\dfrac{8}{7}$ _____

Divide the fractions. Give all answers in mixed number form.

24. $\dfrac{2}{3} \div \dfrac{3}{4}$ _____ **25.** $2\dfrac{1}{2} \div \dfrac{3}{4}$ _____

Write the equivalent decimal.

26. $\dfrac{3}{4}$ _____ **27.** $2\dfrac{7}{8}$ _____

NAME _____

DATE _____

Write as percents.

1. $\frac{1}{2}$ _____   2. $\frac{3}{4}$ _____

3. $\frac{5}{8}$ _____   4. $\frac{4}{5}$ _____

Write the percents as fractions.

5. 40% _____   6. 12.5% _____

7. $33\frac{1}{3}\%$ _____   8. 125% _____

Find the given percent.

9. Find 24% of 200. _____   10. Find 45% of 90. _____

11. 75% of 125 is _____ .   12. 120% of 18 is _____ .

13. $66\frac{2}{3}\%$ of 36 is _____ .   14. Find 62.5% of 64. _____

Find the number whose given percent is given.

15. 45% of what number is 45? _____   16. 90% of what number is 81? _____

17. 40% of what number is 64? _____   18. 110% of what number is 77? _____

19. $33\frac{1}{3}\%$ of what number is 75? _____   20. 75% of what number is 150? _____

21. 37.5% of what number is $\frac{1}{4}$? _____

Find what percent of one number the other number is.

22. 45 is what percent of 50? _____   23. 85 is what percent of 255? _____

24. 60 is what percent of 75? _____   25. 32 is what percent of 48? _____

26. 54 is what percent of 45? _____

1. Name 4 arithmetic operations. _____

2. What does "evaluate" mean? _____

Evaluate.

3. $(9 + 7) \times 6$ _____

4. $9 + (7 \times 6)$ _____

5. $19 + (51 + 37)$ _____

6. $(19 + 51) + 37$ _____

7. $88 - (19 + 14)$ _____

8. $(88 - 19) + 14$ _____

9. $12 \times (6 \div 2)$ _____

10. $(12 \times 6) \div 2$

11. $12 \div (6 \times 2)$ _____

12. $(12 \div 6) \times 2$ _____

13. $36 - [18 - (7 + 3)]$ _____

14. $(36 - 18) - (7 + 3)$ _____

15. $[36 - (18 - 7)] + 3$ _____

16. $\dfrac{6 \times 8}{2 + 8} + 4$ _____

17. $[(6 \times 8) \div (2 + 8)] + 4$ _____

18. $[(6 \div 2) + (8 \div 8)] + 4$ _____

19. $24 \times [(8 \div 2) - 2]$ _____

20. $[(24 \times 8) \div 2] - 2$ _____

21. Change $\dfrac{7}{8}$ into a decimal. _____

22. Change 0.125 into a percent. _____

23. Three fourths of 24 is _____ .

24. $26 \times$ _____ $= 312$

25. Write $23\dfrac{5}{6}$ as an improper fraction. _____

NAME _____

DATE _____

Write an expression representing the quantity described.

1. The sum of 6 and *d* _____

2. The difference of 6 minus *d* _____

3. The product of 6 and *d* _____

4. The quotient of 6 divided by *d* _____

5. Seven plus one half of *x* _____

6. Seven plus twice *x* _____

7. Define: variable _____

8. What does "to substitute" a value for a variable mean? _____

9. What does "evaluate an expression" mean? _____

Evaluate by substituting the given value of the variable.

10. $3 + x$ if *x* is   **a.** 4 _____   **b.** 3.5 _____

11. $8y$ if *y* is   **a.** 3.5 _____   **b.** $2\frac{1}{2}$ _____

12. $\dfrac{6 + x}{4}$ if *x* is   **a.** 4 _____   **b.** 14 _____

Write an expression for the length marked "?".

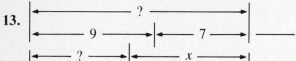

13.

14.

15.

16.

Perform the indicated operations.

17. $\dfrac{5}{6} + \dfrac{3}{4}$ _____   **18.** $\dfrac{5}{6} \times \dfrac{3}{4}$ _____

19. $\dfrac{5}{6} - \dfrac{3}{4}$ _____   **20.** $\dfrac{5}{6} \div \dfrac{3}{4}$ _____

21. What is the least common multiple of 6 and 4? _____

22. What is the greatest common factor of 6 and 4? _____

1. In the expression 4^5 the 4 is called the _____, the 5 is called

the _____, and the whole expression is called a _____.

Evaluate.

2. 2^3 _____ **3.** 3^2 _____

4. 2^5 _____ **5.** 5^2 _____

6. $\left(\dfrac{3}{4}\right)^2$ _____

7. a. Write 81 as a product of 3's. _____ **8. a.** Write 64 as a product of 2's. _____
  b. Replace the ? in   **b.** Replace the ? in

  $81 = 3^?$ _____ $64 = 2^?$ _____

9. a. Write 64 as a product of 4's. _____ **10. a.** Write 64 as a product of 8's. _____
  b. Replace the ? in   **b.** Replace the ? in

  $64 = 4^?$ _____ $64 = 8^?$ _____

Evaluate.

11. Five cubed _____ **12.** Seven squared _____

13. Ten to the fifth _____ **14.** Three to the third power _____

15. One tenth to the second _____

Solve.

16. $11\dfrac{1}{2} \times 3$ _____ **17.** $11\dfrac{1}{2} - 2\dfrac{3}{4}$ _____

18. 24 plus an increase of 50% more is _____.

19. The perimeter of a triangle with sides of length 6, 4, and 8 is

_____ .

20. The area of a square of side x is _____ .

1. List the order in which operations in an expression are to be performed.

_____

For each of the following expressions, evaluate using the correct order of operations.

2. $8 - 6 + 4 \times 2$ _____

3. $8 \times 6 - 4 \times 2$ _____

4. $8 \times (6 - 4) \times 2$ _____

5. $8 \times 6 \div 4 \times 2$ _____

6. $8 \times 6 \div (4 \times 2)$ _____

7. $2^3 - 5 + 4$ _____

8. $12 + 6 - 4^2$ _____

9. $2^4 \times 5 - 3$ _____

10. $2^4 \times (5 - 3)$ _____

11. $2 \div 4 \times 6 + 8$ _____

Evaluate each of the following expressions for the given value of the variable.

12. x^2 if x is **a.** 6 _____

b. 0.2 _____

13. $x^2 + 3$ if x is **a.** 6 _____

b. 0.2 _____

14. $x^2 - 3x + 2$ if x is **a.** 4 _____

b. 5 _____

15. $4x^2 + 3x + 2$ if x is **a.** 3 _____

b. 5 _____

c. 0.2 _____

Solve.

16. 75% of _____ is 24.

17. $\frac{2}{3}$ of _____ is 81.

18. $12\frac{2}{3} - 10\frac{3}{4} =$ _____

19. $8.5 - 6 - 0.25 =$ _____

20. John mowed one third of a 1200 square foot lawn. Then he mowed four fifths of what remained. How many square feet of lawn remained unmowed after this?

_____

SKILLS PRACTICE 7

For use with Section 1-5
Expressions from Word Statements

Write an expression for the quantity described. Use parentheses only when necessary.

1. The sum of 8 and y _____

2. The sum of 8 and y plus 3 _____

3. Twice the sum of 8 and y _____

4. One half the sum of 8 and y _____

5. Add 7 to the product of 6 and x. _____

6. Divide the sum of 5 and x by 3. _____

7. Divide 3 by the sum of 5 and x. _____

8. Subtract 9 from the product of 5 and y. _____

9. Subtract the product of 5 and y from 9. _____

10. The sum of the squares of 5 and x _____

11. The square of the sum of 5 and x _____

12. Add 6 and x, then subtract 8 from the result. _____

13. Add 6 and x, then subtract that result from 8. _____

14. Square the quantity y plus x. _____

15. Five times the product of 4 and x _____

16. Five times the sum of 4 and x _____

17. Subtract the square of 5 from the product of 6 and y. _____

18. Add 7 and x then multiply the result by 8. _____

19. Multiply 7 and x, then add 8 to the result. _____

20. The quantity 6 minus y plus the quantity 4 plus y _____

Solve.

21. $11x + 3$ if x is 3.4 _____

22. $(11 - 4)^2 - 5 \cdot 3$ _____

23. _____% of 126 is 84. _____

24. Change $\frac{5}{6}$ into a percent. _____

1. a. Write an equation which states that the expression $x + 3$ equals 18.

_____

   b. Solve the equation which you wrote in part a. _____

2. For the expression $x - 8$

   a. evaluate the expression for $x = 37$. _____

   b. find the value of x if the expression equals 37. _____

3. For the expression $8x$

   a. evaluate the expression for $x = 24$. _____

   b. find the value of x if the expression equals 24. _____

   c. find the value of x if the expression equals 18. _____

Solve each of the following equations. Show the transformation step.

4. $x + 8 = 15$ _____

5. $x - 14 = 25$ _____

6. $x - 64 = 81$ _____

7. $x + 64 = 81$ _____

8. $6x = 42$ _____

9. $4x = 30$ _____

10. $8x = 54$ _____

11. $\frac{1}{8}x = 54$ _____

12. $\frac{1}{4}x = 24.4$ _____

13. $0.3x = 15$ _____

14. $\left(\frac{2}{3}\right)x = 9$ _____

15. $x - \frac{4}{5} = 2\frac{2}{5}$ _____

Solve.

16. Evaluate $3x^2 - 4x + 5$ if x is 2. _____

17. If $32 = 2^?$, then the ? is _____ .

18. Evaluate $[(4 + 5) \div 3 \cdot 2] + 3^4$. _____

19. 78.34 divided by 100 is _____ .

20. List the multiples of 3 from 3 to 21. _____

1. For the given rectangle, write an expression for each of the
   following:

   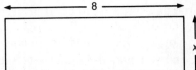

   a. the perimeter _____

   b. the area _____

2. Define   **a.** perimeter of a figure _____

   b. area of a figure _____

3. Consider the given rectangle.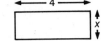

   a. Write an expression for the perimeter. _____

   b. Evaluate the expression in part a if x is 6. _____

   c. What is the perimeter of the rectangle if x is 6? _____

   d. Write an equation which states that the perimeter is 28. _____

   e. Write an expression for the area of the rectangle. _____

   f. Evaluate the expression in part e if x is 6. _____

   g. What is the area of the rectangle if x is 6? _____

   h. What is the area of the rectangle if x is 8? _____

   i. Write an equation which states that the area is 28. _____

   j. Solve the equation in part i to find the width if the area is 28. _____

   k. Find the width if the area is 56. _____

4. What is the difference between evaluating an expression and
   solving a equation?
   _____

   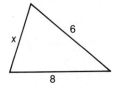

5. **a.** Find the perimeter of the given triangle if x is 8. _____

   b. Find x if the perimeter of the rectangle is 27. _____

6. **a.** Find the area of the given rectangle if x is 4.5. _____

   b. Find x if the area is 36. _____

Solve.

7. $6\frac{5}{6} \times 8\frac{1}{2} =$ _____

8. $6\frac{5}{6} \div 8\frac{1}{2} =$ _____

9. Write an expression for 7 minus the product of 5 and x. _____

10. **a.** $\frac{3}{4} + \frac{7}{4} =$ _____

   b. $\frac{3}{4} \times \frac{7}{4} =$ _____

Foerster *Algebra I*   9

SKILLS PRACTICE 10

For use with Section 1-9
Problems That Lead to Expressions and
Equations

NAME _____

DATE _____

Write an expression to describe each of the following.

1. You and your friend are running together. If you run for x minutes and you started 3 minutes before your friend, in terms of x, how many minutes has your friend run? _____

2. Jane gets $6.50 more allowance each week than her brother John. If John get d dollars, in terms of d, how much does Jane get? _____

For Problems 3 and 4, do the following:

Define and label a variable.
Write an expression to describe the situation.
Either evaluate the expression or write an equation and solve in order
to answer the question asked.

3. Charles wants to dig a rectangular flower bed which is twice as long as it is wide. Let x be the number of feet in width.
   a. Write the definition of x. _____

   b. Write an expression for the length of the flower bed. _____

   c. If the flower bed is 2 feet wide, how long is it? _____

   d. Write an equation which states that the bed is 12 feet long. _____

   e. Solve the equation to find the width of the flower bed. _____
   f. If you are given a width for the rectangle, would you evaluate the expression or write an equation and solve in order to find the length? _____

4. Paul normally spends about 45 cents more on his lunch than his friend Stephanie.

   a. Define a variable for the amount Paul spends on lunch. _____

   b. Write an expression for the amount Stephanie spends. _____
   c. How much does Paul spend when Stephanie spends $1.35, $2.25? _____
   d. How much does Stepahnie spend when Paul spends $3.14, $2.37? _____

5. You have read 75 pages of a 250 page book. What percent of the book remains unread? _____

6. A recipe calls for 2 parts mix, 1 part sugar, and 5 parts water. What percent of the final mixture is sugar? _____

7. There are 5280 feet in a mile. Change 900 feet per minute to miles per hour. Round the answer to the nearest one-hundredth. _____

8. Evaluate $2^3 + [54 - (13 - 8)]$. _____

9. Write $24\frac{5}{12}$ as a decimal. _____

Evaluate.

1. $8 \cdot 5 + 8 \div 4 + (9 - 3)$ _____

2. $3^2 - 7 + 5 \cdot 7$ _____

3. $\dfrac{12 + 6}{9 + 3}$ _____   4. $\dfrac{12}{9} + \dfrac{6}{3}$ _____

5. $6.25(10^5)$ _____

6. $8 \div 4 \cdot 2 - 7 + 3$ _____

7. $2 + 3(8 + 4)$ _____

8. $4x^2 - 5x + 3$ if x is **a.** 3 _____   **b.** 0.3 _____

9. For the expression $x + 12$
   a. Evaluate the expression if x is 28. _____

   b. Find the value of x if the expression is 28. _____

10. Write 343 as a power with 7 as the base. _____

11. Write $b \cdot b \cdot b \cdot b \cdot b$ as a power. _____

12. Write an expression for each of the following.

   a. x plus 8 minus 3 _____

   b. The quantity 9 minus y, squared _____

   c. Subtract 6 from x, then multiply the result by 5. _____

   d. The sum of the cubes of x and 4 _____

   e. The cube of the sum of x and 4 _____

   f. Add 17 to the product of 3 and z. _____

13. When writing tests for students, teachers generally expect students to take about 2.3 times as long to work a test as the teacher.
   a. Define a variable for how many minutes a teacher takes on a test. Write an expression in terms of that variable for how many minutes it will take the students.

   _____

   b. How long will students take if the teacher takes 15 minutes, 21 minutes?

   _____

   c. If the students finish the test in about 55 minutes, about how long would it take the teacher to do the test?

   _____

Write an example for each of the following:

1. A positive integer _____

2. A positive non-integer _____

3. A real number which is neither positive nor negative _____

4. Two numbers whose sum is positive _____

5. Two numbers whose sum is negative _____

6. A positive number and a negative number whose sum is positive

_____

7. A positive number and a negative number whose sum is negative

_____

8. Graph the following numbers on a number line:

a. 0 _____

b. -2 _____

c. 3 _____

d. 4.5 _____

e. $-2\frac{2}{3}$ _____

9. Write an expression for the square of the sum of x and 3.

10. Evaluate $5x^2 - 3x + 2$ if x is 4 _____

11. Evaluate $11\frac{2}{3} - 8\frac{3}{4}$ _____

12. Evaluate $11\frac{2}{3} \cdot 2\frac{2}{5}$ _____

13. What number is 25% more than 24? _____

Evaluate each of the following expressions:

1. $16 + (-12)$ _____

2. $-16 + 12$ _____

3. $-16 + (-12)$ _____

4. $\frac{3}{4} + \left(-\frac{1}{2}\right)$ _____

5. $0.5 + (-.25)$ _____

6. $-18 + 26$ _____

7. $-12 + (-24)$ _____

8. $56 + (-89)$ _____

9. $-89 + 56$ _____

10. $-56 + (-89)$ _____

11. $-34 + (-25)$ _____

12. $8 + (-8)$ _____

13. $-8 + 8$ _____

14. $-8 + (-8)$ _____

15. $|-17|$ _____

16. $|12|$ _____

17. $2 + (-3) + 4$ _____

18. $12 + 6 + (-8) + (-4)$ _____

19. $-37 + 45 + (-25)$ _____

20. $-23 + 67 + (-48)$ _____

21. One fourth of one half of 32 is _____.

22. If there are 2 pints to a quart and 4 quarts to a gallon, how many pints are there in 2.5 gallons of juice?

_____

23. Evaluate $3 \cdot 4^2 + 4(8 - 3)$. _____

24. a. Write an expression for the area of a rectangle with sides of 4 and x.

_____

b. Find x if the area is 26. _____

c. Did you solve or evaluate to find the answer to part b?

_____

25. Solve and check:
a. $x - 4 = 24$ _____
b. $4x = 24$ _____

26. Write an expression with 2 terms in which one term is a variable.

_____

Evaluate.

1. $8 - 5$ _____

2. $5 - 8$ _____

3. $-8 - 5$ _____

4. $-8 + 5$ _____

5. $10 - (-3)$ _____

6. $-7 - (-4)$ _____

7. $76 - (-23)$ _____

8. $-37 - 14$ _____

9. $0 - 15$ _____

10. $-23 - (-45)$ _____

11. $(8 - 12) - (17 - 4)$ _____

12. $[6 - (5 - 9)] - (-25)$ _____

13. $-12 + 5 + 12 - 5$ _____

14. $-17 - (-17)$ _____

15. $-(-(-(-5)))$ _____

16. $3.4 - 8$ _____

17. $-1.4 + 6$ _____

18. $-3\frac{1}{2} - 2\frac{3}{4}$ _____

19. $14 - 16 - (-67) + 16$ _____

20. $23 - x$ if x is   **a.** $5.$ _____   **b.** $-5.$ _____   **c.** $15.$ _____   **d.** $-15.$ _____

21. $|7 - 11|$ _____

22. $|11 - 7|$ _____

23. $-|14 - 5| - 8$ _____

24. Change $\frac{7}{8}$ into a percent. _____

25. If you get 18 out of 20 problems on a test correct, what percent
of the test have you done correctly?

_____

26. $1.2 (\underline{\quad}) = 6.72$ _____

27. Write as a number: Ten million four thousand thirty-seven and
forty-five hundredths.

_____

28. Factor into primes: 72. _____

Evaluate.

1. $(-2)(4)$ _____

2. $(-2)(-4)$ _____

3. $2(-4)$ _____

4. $(-2)^3$ _____

5. -2^3 _____

6. $(-3)^4$ _____

7. -3^4 _____

8. $(-3)(5)(-8)$ _____

9. $(-4)(-5)(-6)$ _____

10. $6(8)(-9)$ _____

11. $-6(0.5)(-8)$ _____

12. $(-2)^2(-3)^3$ _____

13. Evaluate $(-2)^x$ if x is **a.** 1 _____

b. 2 _____

c. 3 _____

d. 4 _____

e. 5 _____

14. a. Evaluate $-x$ if x is **i.** 4 _____

ii. -4 _____

b. Evaluate $-1 \cdot x$ if x is **i.** 4 _____

ii. -4 _____

15. a. $(4)(9) =$ _____

b. $(4)(-9) =$ _____

c. $(-4)(-9) =$ _____

d. $(-4)(9) =$ _____

e. $-4 + (-9) =$ _____

f. $-4 + 9 =$ _____

g. $4 - 9 =$ _____

h. $4 + (-9) =$ _____

16. Write an expression for the sum of the squares of x and y.

_____

17. Write an expression for 8 subtracted from the product of 9 and x.

_____

18. Write an expression for the quotient of the quantity 6 plus x divided by the product of 5 and y.

_____

19. Evaluate $2^3 - 4 \cdot 2 + 16$. _____

1. What is the opposite of -2? _____ What is the reciprocal of -2? _____

2. Using x and y, state the definition of division. _____

3. Fill in the following table with the missing numbers.

original number	opposite	reciprocal
3	-3	$\frac{1}{3}$
-4		$-\frac{1}{4}$
$\frac{1}{5}$	$-\frac{1}{5}$	
$-\frac{2}{3}$		
	8	
		-6
0		has none

Evaluate.

4. $\dfrac{-18}{9}$ _____

5. $\dfrac{-18}{-9}$ _____

6. $-\dfrac{(-27)}{-3}$ _____

7. $-\dfrac{18}{-6}$ _____

8. $\dfrac{(8)(-7)}{14}$ _____

9. $\dfrac{(-4)(-6)(3)}{(-12)(-3)}$ _____

10. $-\dfrac{3(-4)}{2}$ _____

11. $\dfrac{8-8}{15}$ _____

12. $\dfrac{-9+9}{7}$ _____

13. $\dfrac{15}{8-8}$ _____

14. $\dfrac{-28}{0}$ _____

15. $\dfrac{90}{50}$ _____

16. Evaluate $\dfrac{12+x}{x}$ if x is   a. -4 _____   b. -12 _____   c. 0 _____

17. Evaluate $\dfrac{4-x}{x-4}$ if x is   a. -4 _____   b. 4 _____   c. -8 _____

18. $\dfrac{-15}{x}$ if x is   a. 3 _____   b. -3 _____   c. 0 _____

19. $-\dfrac{8x}{2(-3)}$ if x is   a. -12 _____   b. 4 _____

20. $\dfrac{-2}{x}$ if x is   a. 1 _____   b. -1 _____   c. 0 _____

21. Solve for x: $x + 17 = 28$ ____   22. Solve for x: $4x = 24$ ____   23. Solve for x: $0.5x = 6$ ____

Evaluate. Follow the correct order of operations.

1. $(-3)(-5) - 6$ _____

2. $-6 - 4(-8)$ _____

3. $[(-3) - (-5)(6)] - 4$ _____

4. $-5(16 - 12)$ _____

5. $6 - 2^3$ _____

6. $\dfrac{8 - 24}{-4} - (-11)$ _____

7. $4(-3)^2 - 6(-3) - 16$ _____

8. $\dfrac{-18}{-4} - \dfrac{34}{2}$ _____

9. $18 - 3[(-24) + 16]$ _____

10. $(-3)\,4 - 45 + 36$ _____

11. $15(-9) + 2^4(7 - 10)$ _____

12. $\dfrac{4 - 6(8 - 14)}{10}$ _____

13. $(-2)(3)(-4) - 8 + 6$ _____

14. $1 - 2 + 3 - 4 + \dfrac{5(6)}{-3} + (-3)^2$ _____

15. $\dfrac{12 + 4}{4 - 12}$ _____

Evaluate for the given values of the variable.

16. $\dfrac{2x - 4}{2 + x}$ for $x =$

    a. -6 _____
    b. 6 _____
    c. -2 _____
    d. 2 _____

17. $3x^2 - 4x + 6$ for $x =$

    a. 4 _____
    b. -4 _____

Solve. The transformations and the solutions could involve negative numbers.

18. $-4x = 24$ _____

19. $x - (-4) = 6$ _____

20. $3x = -21$ _____

21. $\left(-\dfrac{2}{3}\right)x = 12$ _____

22. $x + 8 = -6$ _____

23. $-8x = -46$ _____

24. $x - 18 = -13$ _____

Simplify by commuting and associating.

1. $3 + y + 8$ _____

2. $5 + x - 7$ _____

3. $-4 + y + 6$ _____

4. $-12 + 3x - 8$ _____

5. $14 - x - 9$ _____

6. $10 - 2x + 7$ _____

7. $-4 - 5x - 6$ _____

8. $2 \cdot x \cdot 5$ _____

9. $8 \cdot y(-4)$ _____

10. $(4x)(-6)$ _____

11. $5x \cdot 4$ _____

12. $(-7x)(8)$ _____

13. $-16x(-2)$ _____

14. $\left(-\dfrac{3}{4}\right) \cdot x \cdot (-8)$ _____

15. $\dfrac{-12x}{2}$ _____

16. $\dfrac{18x}{-9}$ _____

17. $\dfrac{-24x}{-4}$ _____

18. $32x\left(-\dfrac{7}{8}\right)$ _____

19. $\dfrac{-x}{-1}$ _____

20. $-28x \div (-7)$ _____

21. Evaluate $|4 + x|$ if x is

    a. 7 _____   **b.** -7 _____

22. Write 64 as a power of 2. _____

23. Write an expression to describe 8 times x plus 3. _____

24. Evaluate $\dfrac{12 - 8}{4 - 2}$. _____

25. What number is 8 less than twice 6? _____

Solve. Show all transformation steps.

1. $2x + 3 = 9$ _____

2. $4x - 6 = 10$ _____

3. $6x + 8 = -16$ _____

4. $-8x + 32 = -16$ _____

5. $5 - 4x = -7$ _____

6. $-6 - 3x = 24$ _____

7. $12 - x = 3$ _____

8. $8x - 9 = -27$ _____

9. $5x + 3 = -78$ _____

10. $12x - 8 = 28$ _____

11. $-24 = 8 - 8x$ _____

12. $\left(-\frac{2}{3}\right)x + 6 = -4$ _____

13. $17 = 8 - x$ _____

14. $8x - 3 = -11$ _____

15. $7 - 2x = 17$ _____

16. $3 - 9x = -36$ _____

17. $0.5x + 1.2 = -2.3$ _____

18. $9 - x = -9$ _____

19. $17 - x = 0$ _____

20. $3x - 3 = -12$ _____

21. Write an expression to describe: Subtract 8 from the product of x and 3.

_____

22. Write an expression to describe: Subtract the product of x and 3 from 8.

_____

23. Write the prime factors of 24. _____

24. Evaluate $5 - x$ if x is

    a. 9 _____   **b.** -9 _____

25. Evaluate $\dfrac{5 - x}{x - 5}$ if x is

    a. 5 _____   **b.** -5 _____

SKILLS PRACTICE 20
For use with Section 2-8
Problems That Lead to Two-Transformation
Equations

NAME _____

DATE _____

For Problems 1 and 2:
Label the variable. Write and label an expression. *Without changing the expression* either evaluate the expression if the value of the variable is given or write an equation and solve for the variable if the value of the expression is given.

1. Manuel found that he averaged 4 min. per equation when he solved equations on his homework. But it took him 5 min. to get his work area organized so he could do his work. Therefore, the number of min. he spent on solving equations and organization time would be 4 times the number of equations plus 5.

   If x = the number of equations solved, then $4x + 5$ = the total number of minutes spent on homework and organization.

   a. If he solved 7 equations, how much time did he spend total on his algebra homework?

      _____

   b. Set up an equation which states that Manuel spent 37 minutes on homework.

      _____

   c. Solve the equation to find the total number of problems done.

      _____

   d. Manuel was assigned 12 problems to solve and he worked for 45 minutes. Did he finish the assignment? Justify your answer.

2. Patrick has $5.45 (545 cents) in his pocket. He goes to the convenience store to buy some chips, and the small bags cost $0.45 each (including tax). For each bag of chips he buys, he has $0.45 (45 cents) less in his pocket.
   Let b = the number of bags of chips Patrick buys.
   a. Write an expression to describe the number of cents Patrick has left after buying b bags of chips.
   b. How many bags does he buy if he has $1.85 left?
   c. Did you evaluate the expression or write and solve an equation to get the answer to part b? If you did neither, do that part again and either evaluate the expression or solve an equation.
   d. How much does he have left if he buys 12 bags of chips?
   e. Patrick wants to buy each of his 15 teammates a bag of chips. Use your expression to determine whether or not this is possible with the money he has in his pocket. Justify your answer with numbers. Please answer in complete sentences.

      _____

      _____

3. Evaluate $[-8 - 3(2 - 5) + 2^3] + 16.$ _____

4. $2\frac{2}{3} - 5\frac{1}{2} =$ _____   5. $8.5 - 26 =$ _____   6. Evaluate $\dfrac{-24.5}{0.05}.$ _____

SKILLS PRACTICE 21
Chapter 2 Review
Operations with Negative Numbers

NAME _____

DATE _____

Evaluate.

1. $-3(5 - 8)$ _____

2. $6 - (-8)$ _____

3. $6(-8)$ _____

4. $(-2)^2 + 15 - 18$ _____

5. $\dfrac{-24 + 28}{8 - 6}$ _____

6. $(-3 - 5)(-5 + 8)$ _____

7. $-12 \cdot 3 + 8(-6) - 9$ _____

8. $-3^2 - 24 - 6(-5)$ _____

9. $7 - (8 - 14)$ _____

10. $\dfrac{36 - 48}{-9} + 4$ _____

11. $|15 - 7|$ _____

12. $|7 - 15|$ _____

13. $(-2)^4 - 2^4$ _____

14. $3(-4) - (-6)$ _____

15. Evaluate $3x^2 - 5x + 4$ if x is **a.** 1 _____ **b.** -1 _____

16. Evaluate $\dfrac{3x - 6}{x + 2}$ if x is **a.** -2 _____ **b.** 2 _____

Simplify by commuting and associating.

17. $3 + x - 8$ _____

18. $-6 - x + 19$ _____

19. $15x \cdot 3$ _____

20. $-18x \div (-3)$ _____

Solve. Show all transformation steps.

21. $2x - 4 = -8$ _____

22. $9 - x = 15$ _____

23. $7x + 5 = -9$ _____

24. $6 - 3x = -9$ _____

25. Joan can ride her bike at an average of 4 minutes per mile. It takes her about 6 minutes to get her bicycle out, get ready to ride, and put her bike up after the ride.

Let m be the number of miles she rides.

a. i. Write the definition of m. _____
   ii. Write an expression for how many minutes it takes her to pedal m miles. _____
   iii. If you add 6 minutes to the answer in part ii, the resulting expression will represent the total number of minutes a ride takes. Write this expression and label it "total number of minutes a ride takes." _____

b. If Joan rode 11 mi., how many min. total did the ride take? _____

c. If Joan's ride took a total of 1 h., 42 min., how far did she ride? _____

d. How many miles per hour was Joan pedalling? _____

Simplify by distributing the multiplication over the addition or subtraction.

1. $3(x + 6)$ _____

2. $5(x - 8)$ _____

3. $-6(x - 5)$ _____

4. $-3(x + 3)$ _____

5. $x(x + 2)$ _____

6. $x(2x + 4)$ _____

7. $\frac{1}{3}(6x - 18)$ _____

8. $\frac{3}{2}\left(4x + \frac{4}{3}\right)$ _____

9. $\left(-\frac{3}{4}\right)(8x - 6)$ _____

10. $\left(-\frac{2}{3}\right)\left(3x + \frac{2}{3}\right)$ _____

Simplify by distributing, commuting, and associating.

11. $3 + 2(x + 5)$ _____

12. $5 + 3(x - 4)$ _____

13. $4(6 - x) + 7$ _____

14. $5(8x - 5) - 3$ _____

15. $7 + 2(8 - x)$ _____

16. $-5(x - 6) - 4$ _____

17. $2(3x + 4) - 5$ _____

18. $-4(2x + 4) - 6$ _____

19. $5(6 - x) - 8$ _____

20. $4 + 5(6x + 7)$ _____

Solve and check Exercises 21−25.

21. $2x - 5 = 8$ _____

22. $x - 9 = 17$ _____

23. $17 - 3x = 14$ _____

24. $8 + 2x = 8$ _____

25. $9x + 18 = 0$ _____

Simplify by distributing multiplication or division over addition or subtraction. Write in lowest terms.

1. $2(3x + 4)$ _____

2. $2(3x - 4)$ _____

3. $-1(7 + x)$ _____

4. $-(7 - x)$ _____

5. $\frac{1}{2}(4x + 6)$ _____

6. $\frac{4x + 6}{2}$ _____

7. $(8x - 5) \cdot 7$ _____

8. $(3 - 4x)(-6)$ _____

9. $\frac{6x - 4}{-2}$ _____

10. $3(x - y + 7)$ _____

11. $(-3)(2x - 4y - 6)$ _____

12. $(2x - 4y - 6)(-3)$ _____

13. $-(8 - x)$ _____

14. $-(x - 8)$ _____

15. $-1(6x - 5)$ _____

16. $-(6x - 5)$ _____

17. $(-8 + 6x)(-4)$ _____

18. $(4 + 6x - 5y) \cdot 2$ _____

19. $\frac{8x - 6y + 9}{-2}$ _____

20. $8\left(\frac{1}{2} + \frac{3}{4}x\right)$ _____

Simplify exercises by commuting and associating.

21. $5 - 6x + 3$ _____

22. $-8 + 5x - 9$ _____

23. $9 - x - 6$ _____

24. $5 + 4y - 8$ _____

25. $3 + 7x + 4$ _____

Combine like terms.

1. $2x + 3x$ _____

2. $2x - 5x$ _____

3. $-4x + 9x$ _____

4. $-3x - 5x$ _____

5. $4x + 2x - 2$ _____

6. $7x - x$ _____

7. $5 - 5x + 8x$ _____

8. $5 - 5x + 8$ _____

Simplify by distributing and combining like terms.

9. $2(3x + 5) - 5x$ _____

10. $2(x - 5) + 3$ _____

11. $8 - 2(7x + 3)$ _____

12. $8 - 2(7x - 3)$ _____

13. $5 - 1(3x + 4)$ _____

14. $5 - (3x + 4)$ _____

15. $-4 - 3(4x - 5)$ _____

16. $-5(4x + 2) - 8$ _____

17. $-(4 - x) + 6$ _____

18. $9 + 2(3x + 4)$ _____

19. $9 - 2(-3x - 4)$ _____

20. $4 - 2(x + 4) - 3(5x - 2)$ _____

Write expressions to describe the given situations.

21. You have x cents, then you spend 35 cents. How much do you now have?

_____

22. You are y years old. Your little brother is three fourths of your age. How old is your little brother?

_____

23. There are twice as many freshmen in your class as there are sophomores. If there are s sophomores, how many freshmen are there?

_____

24. Evaluate $2(x - 4)$ if x is

a. -3 _____   **b.** 9 _____

25. Evaluate $2x^2 - 3x + 5$ if x is

a. -2 _____   **b.** 2 _____

Simplify by distributing and combining like terms.

1. $3 - (x - 4)$ _____

2. $5x - x + 3(x + 5)$ _____

3. $4 - 4x(x + 6) - 8$ _____

4. $5(x + 3) - 3x(2x - 8)$ _____

5. $4x^2 - 3x^2 + 5x - x^2 - 1$ _____

6. $5 - 6x(5 - x) + 4(x + 3)$ _____

7. $4x^2 - 3x + 7 + 6x^2 + 7x - 9$ _____

8. $2(3x^2 + 5x - 3) - (x^2 - 6x + 7)$ _____

9. $5(x - 3) + 5x(4x - 5)$ _____

10. $8x - (x^2 - 8x) + 8$ _____

11. $x^3 + y^3 - 4x^2 + 8x^2 - 5x + 6x + 9$ _____

12. $8(x - 9) - 4(3x - 6)$ _____

13. $4x^2 - (5x^2 - 8x) + 9x$ _____

14. $(3x - 8) \cdot (-3) - (3x - 6)$ _____

15. $8 - (7 - x) + 3x - 9$ _____

16. $x(2y + 3) - 5xy + 7x$ _____

17. $y(x + 4) + 4(y - 8)$ _____

18. $3x(3x + 5) + 5(3x + 5)$ _____

19. $x(x - 5) + 5(x - 5)$ _____

20. $5x(5x + 2) - 2(5x + 2)$ _____

SKILLS PRACTICE 26
For use with Section 3-5
Axioms for Adding and Multiplying

NAME _____

DATE _____

Use the following axioms and definitions to justify the statements.

Axioms of Operations
Commutative axiom of addition
Commutative axiom of multiplication
Associative axiom of addition
Associative axiom of multiplication
Additive identity
Additive inverse
Multiplicative identity
Multiplicative inverse
Distributive

Axioms of Equality
Transitive
Symmetric
Reflexive

Definitions
Definition of subtraction
Definition of division

1. $2 + 3 = 3 + 2$ _____

2. If $4 + 3 = 7$, then $7 = 4 + 3$. _____

3. $3 + (-3) = 0$ _____

4. $3 + 0 = 3$ _____

5. $2 - 3 = 2 + (-3)$ _____

6. $2 + (3 + 8) = (2 + 3) + 8$ _____

7. $3(4) = (4)(3)$ _____

8. If $4 + 3 = 7$ and $7 = 2 + 5$, then $4 + 3 = 2 + 5$. _____

9. $5(4 + x) = 20 + 5x$ _____

10. $x = 1 \cdot x$ _____

11. $x \cdot \left(\dfrac{1}{x}\right) = 1$ _____

12. $\dfrac{x}{y} = x \cdot \left(\dfrac{1}{y}\right)$ _____

13. $5(x - 6) = (x - 6) \cdot 5$ _____

14. $5(x - 6) = 5[x + (-6)]$ _____

15. $2x + 4y = 2(x + 2y)$ _____

16. $(2 \cdot 3)(4) = (2)(3 \cdot 4)$ _____

17. $6 + 0 = 6 + 0$ _____

18. $2 + 3x + 5 = 2 + 5 + 3x$ _____

19. $2 + 5 + 3x = (2 + 5) + 3x$ _____

20. $5x + 3x = (5 + 3) \cdot x$ _____

Simplify by distributing and combining like terms.

21. $5x + 3x$ _____

22. $6 + 5x - 3$ _____

23. $6 + 5(x - 3)$ _____

24. $8 - 3(5 - x)$ _____

25. $6 - (4 - 3x) + 7$ _____

26. $(2)(3 \cdot 5x)$ _____

SKILLS PRACTICE 27
For use with Section 3-5
Axioms for Adding and Multiplying

NAME _____

DATE _____

Use the following axioms, definitions, and properties to justify the statements.

Axioms of Operations	*Definitions*	*Axioms of Equality*
Commutative axiom of addition	Definition of subtraction	Transitive
Commutative axiom of multiplication	Definition of division	Symmetric
Associative axiom of addition	*Properties of Equations*	Reflexive
Associative axiom of multiplication	Multiplication property of equality	
Additive identity	Addition property of equality	
Additive inverse	*Multiplication Property of* -1	
Multiplicative identity		
Multiplicative inverse		
Distributive		

When you combine numbers by adding or multiplying, state "arithmetic."

1. Simplify: $2 + 3x + 4$ (Answer is $3x + 6$.)
   a. $2 + 3x + 4 = 3x + 2 + 4$
   b. $3x + 2 + 4 = 3x + (2 + 4)$
   c. $3x + (2 + 4) = 3x + 6$

2. Simplify: $2 + 3(5x + 4)$
(Answer is $15x + 14$.)
   a. $2 + 3(5x + 4) = 2 + 3(5x) + (3)(4)$
   b. $2 + 3(5x) + (3)(4) = 2 + 15x + 12$
   c. $2 + 15x + 12 = 15x + 2 + 12$
   d. $15x + 2 + 12 = 15x + (2 + 12)$
   e. $15x + (2 + 12) = 15x + 14$

3. Simplify: $2 - (4 + x)$
(Answer is $-2 - x$ or $-x - 2$.)
   a. $2 - (4 + x) = 2 + (-1)(4 + x)$
   b. $2 + (-1)(4 + x) =$
      $2 + (-1)(4) + (-1)(x)$
   c. $2 + (-1)(4) + (-1)(x) =$
      $2 + (-4) + (-x)$
   d. $2 + (-4) + (-x) = [2 + (-4)] + (-x)$
   e. $[2 + (-4)] + (-x) = -2 + (-x)$
   f. $-2 + (-x) = -2 - x$

4. Simplify: $6 + 7x - 4 - 5x$
(Answer is $2x + 2$.)
   a. $6 + 7x - 4 - 5x = 6 + 7x + (-4) - 5x$
   b. $6 + 7x + (-4) - 5x =$
      $6 + (-4) + 7x - 5x$
   c. $6 + (-4) + 7x - 5x =$
      $[6 + (-4)] + (7x - 5x)$
   d. $[6 + (-4)] + (7x - 5x) = 2 + (7x - 5x)$
   e. $2 + (7x - 5x) = 2 + [7x + (-5)x]$
   f. $2 + [7x + (-5)x] = 2 + [7 + (-5)] \cdot x$
   g. $2 + [7 + (-5)] \cdot x = 2 + 2x$
   h. $2 + 2x = 2x + 2$

5. Solve $x + 6 = 9$ (The solution is $x = 3$.)
   a. $(x + 6) + (-6) = 9 + (-6)$
   b. $x + [6 + (-6)] = 9 + (-6)$
   c. $x + 0 = 9 + (-6)$
   d. $x = 9 + (-6)$
   e. $x = 3$

6. Solve: $-4x = 12$ (The solution is $x = -3$.)
   a. $\left(-\frac{1}{4}\right)(-4x) = \left(-\frac{1}{4}\right)(12)$
   b. $\left[\left(-\frac{1}{4}\right)(-4)\right] \cdot x = \left(-\frac{1}{4}\right)(12)$
   c. $1 \cdot x = \left(-\frac{1}{4}\right)(12)$
   d. $x = \left(-\frac{1}{4}\right)(12)$
   e. $x = -3$

Simplify by distributing, commuting, associating, and combining like terms.

1. $5(x - 3)$ _____

2. $\dfrac{5x - 10}{-5}$ _____

3. $(8 - 4x)(-2)$ _____

4. $7 + 2(3x + 4)$ _____

5. $5 - (4 - x)$ _____

6. $\dfrac{6x - 8}{2} + 4x - 9$ _____

7. $5 + 2(x - 3) + 6x$ _____

8. $5x - x + 5$ _____

9. $9x - 9 + 7x$ _____

10. $3(5x - 4) - 2(7 - 4x)$ _____

Use the distributive axiom to factor out common factors.

11. $2x + 4$ _____

12. $6 - 3x$ _____

13. $2x + 2y$ _____

14. $8x - 12$ _____

15. $3 - 6x + 9y$ _____

Justify each statement with an axiom, definition, or property. If you simply added or multiplied, state "arithmetic."

16. Simplify: $5 + 2(x - 3) + 6x$
   a. $5 + 2(x - 3) + 6x =$
   $5 + 2x - 2(3) + 6x$
   b. $5 + 2x - 2(3) + 6x = 5 + 2x - 6 + 6x$
   c. $5 + 2x - 6 + 6x = 5 + 2x + (-6) + 6x$
   d. $5 + 2x + (-6) + 6x =$
   $5 + (-6) + 2x + 6x$

   e. $5 + (-6) + 2x + 6x =$
   $[5 + (-6)] + 2x + 6x$
   f. $[5 + (-6)] + 2x + 6x = -1 + 2x + 6x$
   g. $-1 + 2x + 6x = -1 + (2 + 6) \cdot x$
   h. $-1 + (2 + 6) \cdot x = -1 + 8x$

17. Solve: $x + 6 = -8$
   a. $(x + 6) + (-6) = -8 + (-6)$
   b. $x + [6 + (-6)] = -8 + (-6)$
   c. $x + [6 + (-6)] = -14$

   d. $x + 0 = -14$
   e. $x = -14$

18. Solve: $4x = -24$
   a. $\left(\dfrac{1}{4}\right) \cdot 4x = \left(\dfrac{1}{4}\right)(-24)$
   b. $\left[\left(\dfrac{1}{4}\right)(4)\right] \cdot x = \left(\dfrac{1}{4}\right)(-24)$
   c. $1 \cdot x = \left(\dfrac{1}{4}\right)(-24)$

   d. $x = \left(\dfrac{1}{4}\right)(-24)$
   e. $x = \dfrac{-24}{4}$
   f. $x = -6$

SKILLS PRACTICE 29

For use with Section 4-1
Equations with Like Terms

NAME _____

DATE _____

Solve.

1. $5x + 2x = 21$ _____

2. $5x - 2x = 21$ _____

3. $6x - 5 + 2x = 11$ _____

4. $6x + 5 - 2x = -11$ _____

5. $5x - 5 - x = -17$ _____

6. $8 - 4x = -12$ _____

7. $3x - 9 + 7x = -8$ _____

8. $5x - 0.4 - 0.2x = 4.4$ _____

9. $2x - 2 - x = -2$ _____

10. $8 - 5x - 9 = 19$ _____

State the axiom or definition which makes each of the following statements true.

11. $x + 2 = 2 + x$ _____

12. $2x - 2 = 2x + (-2)$ _____

13. $2x + (-2) + (-x) = 2x + (-x) + (-2)$ _____

14. If $3 = x - 5$, then $x - 5 = 3$. _____

15. $3(x + 2) = 3x + 6$ _____

Evaluate for each of the following values:

16. $\dfrac{2x - 6}{2 - x}$ for

    a. $x = 2$ _____
    b. $x = 3$ _____
    c. $x = -2$ _____

SKILLS PRACTICE 30
For use with Section 4-2
Equations with Like Terms and Distributing

NAME _____

DATE _____

Solve.

1. $5x + 3 = -12$ _____

2. $5x - 3 = -12$ _____

3. $5x + 3 - 7x = -9$ _____

4. $3(x + 2) = 15$ _____

5. $4(x - 5) = -16$ _____

6. $5(2x - 3) = -10$ _____

7. $2 + 3(x + 2) = 11$ _____

8. $2 - 3(x + 2) = 11$ _____

9. $2 - 3(x - 2) = 11$ _____

10. $2 - 1(x + 5) = 17$ _____

11. $2 - (x + 5) = 17$ _____

12. $6 - 1(3x - 4) = -11$ _____

13. $6 - (3x - 4) = -11$ _____

14. $5(x + 6) - 30 = 30$ _____

15. $4 + 2(5x - 8) = -12$ _____

16. $3(2x - 4) + 7x = 14$ _____

17. $4(3x - 5) + 4 = 0$ _____

18. $6(4 - x) - x = -11$ _____

19. $18 = 3x - 2(x - 5)$ _____

20. $21 = 2 + 3x - 3 - x$ _____

Evaluate.

21. $3x^2 - 5x + 4$ if x is

    a. 2 _____   **b.** -2 _____

22. $5 - (x - 5)$ if x is

    a. 2 _____   **b.** -2 _____

23. $8(5 - x)$ if x is

    a. 5 _____   **b.** -5 _____

24. -1^{22} _____

25. $(-1)^{22}$ _____

SKILLS PRACTICE 31

For use with Section 4-3
Equations with Variables in Both Members

NAME _____

DATE _____

Solve.

1. $2x + 6 = x$ _____

2. $2x + 6 = -x$ _____

3. $2x - 6 = -x$ _____

4. $4x + 3 = x + 6$ _____

5. $6x = 3x + 12$ _____

6. $7x - 13 = -6x$ _____

7. $5x + 6 = 3x - 12$ _____

8. $8 - 3x = 2x - 7$ _____

9. $5x = 9x$ _____

10. $5x + 3 = 7x + 3$ _____

11. $2(x + 4) = 18$ _____

12. $3(2x - 5) + 9 = 6$ _____

13. $4x - 5 = 2(x - 6)$ _____

14. $4 - (3x - 8) = 2x - 17$ _____

15. $x - (x - 5) = 2x - 5$ _____

16. $3(x + 2) - 2(x - 4) = 8 - x$ _____

Solve or state an appropriate conclusion.

17. $5(x + 3) = 2x + 3x$ _____

18. $5(x - 3) = 2x + 3(x - 5)$ _____

19. $5(x - 3) = x + 3(x - 5)$ _____

20. $4 - (6x - 8) = 6(x + 2)$ _____

21. $5 + 3(2x - 8) = -2(x - 4) - 8(9 - x)$ _____

22. $5(6x - 9) = 5(9 - 6x)$ _____

23. State the opposite of $-\dfrac{3}{5}$. _____

24. State the reciprocal of $-\dfrac{3}{5}$. _____

25. What number has no reciprocal? Why not? _____

26. For the expression $3x - 4$
   a. evaluate it if x is -5. _____

   b. find the value of x if the expression is -16. _____

   c. find the value of x if the expression is $2x + 8$. _____

27. Write an expression to describe this situation:
Barney has run at 6 miles an hour for x hours. He has a total of 24 miles to run. How much does he have left to go?

_____

The following equations involve calculations which can best be done with the use of a calculator. After you have obtained the solution, put it into the memory of the calculator, then check the solution by working the equation with the memory value. Write an approximate value of the solution by rounding the answer to 2 decimal places.

1. $3x - 9x = 37$ _____

2. $7x + 8x = 45 + 6x$ _____

3. $9.2x - 6.4 = 8.2$ _____

4. $5.6x - 7.3 = 9.2 + 8.7x$ _____

5. $6(3 - 4.5x) = 8.5 - 9x$ _____

6. $8(4 - 3x) = 17x + 15$ _____

7. $9x + 3(4x - 6) = 25 - (x + 3)$ _____

8. $9 - 3(4x - 7) = 5x + 37$ _____

9. $5x - 4(4x - 24) = 97$ _____

10. $4 + 5(2x - 6) = 2(5x + 8)$ _____

Write expressions to describe each situation.

11. You are paid $6 an hour plus an additional $25 for extra work. If you work for x hours, how much do you get paid?

_____

12. You have 76 tickets to sell and you sell them at the rate of about 6 per day. How many tickets do you have left after d days of selling?

_____

13. You have a bag of 24 cookies. Each of your friends grab an average of 2.5 cookies per person. If f of your friends grab cookies, how many cookies do you have left?

_____

14. You have $426 in your savings account. If you save $2.50 a month, how much will you have x years from now?

_____

15. You do not pay tax on the first $5000 you earn. Any earnings after that are taxed at a rate of 20% (.20) of what is earned above the $5000. How much do you get, after taxes, if you earn $6000?

_____

SKILLS PRACTICE 33
For use with Section 4-6
Problems That Involve More Than One
Expression

NAME _____

DATE _____

1. John and Javier are entered in the intramural cookie eating contest. John eats cookies at the rate of 6 cookies per minute while Javier eats them at the rate of 8 cookies per minute. Each person was given a plate which was supposed to have 72 cookies on it. However, someone had miscounted and John's plate had only 50 cookies on it.

   Let m be the number of minutes they have eaten.

   a. i. Write an expression for the number of cookies left on Javier's plate after m minutes. _____

   ii. Write an expression for the number of cookies left on John's plate after m minutes. _____

   b. i. Write an equation which states that they have the same number of cookies on their plates. _____

   ii. Solve the equation in part i to find out how many minutes have passed before they have the same number of cookies remaining. _____

   c. How many cookies does each one have after 1 minute, 2 minutes, 8 minutes? _____

   d. How long before they have 50 cookies remaining? _____

   e. Who won the contest? Justify your answer. _____

2. Than and Sam are reading books for English. Than's book has 235 pages while Sam's book has 358. Than found that she averaged reading 18 pages per hour while Sam averaged about 28. While talking about how long it took them to read their respective books, they found that they read about the same length of time.

   Let h be the number of hours they read.

   a. i. Write an expression for the number of pages Than has read. _____

   ii. Write an expression for the number of pages Than has remaining to be read. _____

   iii. Write an expression for the number of pages Sam has read. _____

   iv. Write an expression for the number of pages Sam has remaining to be read. _____

   b. Who has more left to read after reading 6 hours? How much more? _____

   c. Write an equation which states that Sam has finished his book. (That means 0 pages remaining.) Solve the equation to discover how long it will take him to read his book. _____

   d. Write an equation which states that they have the same number of pages remaining. Solve the equation to find out how many hours this will take. _____

   e. Who finished first? How many pages did the other person have left to read? _____

Solve each of the following equations. Round decimal answers to 2 decimal places.

1. $5x - 7x = 144$ _____

2. $4x - 4 + 5x = 77$ _____

3. $2(x - 5) + 5x = 67$ _____

4. $x + 3(8 - 2x) = -31$ _____

5. $9x - (7 - x) = -67$ _____

6. $8x + 31 = 5x - 41$ _____

7. $2(3x - 4) - x = 3x - 24$ _____

8. $4 - (x - 3) = x + 7$ _____

9. $5 - (4 - 2x) = 2x + 8$ _____

10. $2(3x - 4) - 10 = -15 + 3(2x - 1)$ _____

11. $1.2(3.1x - 4.5) + 8.9 = 3.6x - 7.8$ _____

12. During a local triathalon competition, Jay finished his swimming portion 5 minutes before his nearest competitor, Bill. Therefore, on the next portion, bicycling, Jay started riding 5 minutes before Bill. Jay averaged 0.25 miles per minute on his bicycle ride while Bill averaged 0.3 miles per minute.

Let x be the number of minutes Jay has been riding in the competition.

a. i. Write an expression for the number of miles Jay has ridden after x minutes.

ii. Write an expression, in terms of x, for the number of minutes Bill has been riding.

iii. Write an expression for the number of miles Bill has ridden since Jay started.

b. i. Who is ahead after Jay has been riding for 8 minutes? How far ahead?

ii. Who is ahead after Jay has been riding for 36 minutes? How far ahead?

c. How many minutes will Jay have to ride before Bill catches him?

d. If the bicycling portion of the race is 24 miles, who will complete this portion first, Jay or Bill? How many more minutes will it take the other one to finish?

13. Olivia and Chad were at adjacent typewriters while practicing their typing. Olivia averages 45 words per minute, while Chad averages 36 words per minute. When Olivia started typing, Chad had already typed 90 words. Let x be the number of minutes passed since Olivia started typing.

a. i. Write an expression for the number of words Olivia has typed in x minutes.

ii. Write an expression, in terms of x, for the number of words Chad has typed (including the words typed before Olivia joined him).

b. If Olivia has typed for 5 minutes, how many words have each of them typed?

c. How many minutes did Olivia type before she typed the same number of words as Chad?

Commute terms so that the expression is in descending powers of the variable.

1. $2x^3 - 5 + 3x^2$ _____

2. $5x^4 - 3x^5 + 18 + 4x^3$ _____

3. $x^4 - x^5 + x^2 - x^3$ _____

4. $6x^2 - 5x^4 + 4x^3 + 18x - 24$ _____

5. $8 - 7x^4 + 6x^2 - 5x^3 + 4x$ _____

6. Write $5x^2y^3$ as a product of factors with no exponents other than the understood exponent of 1.

_____

7. Evaluate $3x^2 - 4x + 6$ if x is -2. _____

State the axiom of definition which justifies each statement.

8. $x - y = x + (-y)$ _____

9. $x + y = y + x$ _____

10. If $x = y + 2$ and $y + 2 = z$, then $x = z$. _____

11. $2(x + y) = 2x + 2y$ _____

12. $(a \cdot b) \cdot c = a \cdot (b \cdot c)$ _____

State whether the expression is a polynomial. If not, state the reason.

1. $x^2 + 3x - 2$ _____

2. $\dfrac{x + 7}{5}$ _____

3. $|x + 7|$ _____

4. $3(x + 5^2)$ _____

5. $\dfrac{x^2 + 7}{x}$ _____

Name the polynomials by degree and number of terms.

6. x^2 _____

7. $x + 3$ _____

8. $4x^2 + 3x - 5^3$ _____

9. $6x^3 + 5x^2 + 4x - 8$ _____

10. $x^2 - 25$ _____

11. x _____

12. $x^3 + 2x^2$ _____

13. $7x^2 - 5x + 8$ _____

14. $8x + 5^3$ _____

15. For the polynomial $5x^3 - 4x^2 + x - 7$, state the coefficients of the variables.

_____

Give an example of the polynomial described.

16. A quadratic monomial _____

17. A linear binomial _____

18. A quadratic trinomial _____

19. A cubic polynomial with 4 terms _____

20. a. Give an example of an expression which is a polynomial.

_____

b. Give an example of an expression which is *not* a polynomial.

_____

Simplify each of the following expressions.

21. $5x^2 - 4x + 3x^2 + 6x$ _____

22. $x^2 + 2 - x(x - 4)$ _____

23. $6x^3 + 6x - x^3$ _____

24. $x^2 - 3x^2 + x - 5x + 6$ _____

25. $x(x - 4) - 5(x - 4)$ _____

Multiply the two binomials. Express the resulting polynomials in descending powers of the variables.

1. $(x + 3)(x + 4)$ _____

2. $(x - 4)(x - 5)$ _____

3. $(x + 4)(x - 1)$ _____

4. $(x + 2)(x - 5)$ _____

5. $(x + 2)(x - 5)$ _____

6. $(x - 5)(x + 3)$ _____

7. $(3x - 4)(5x - 2)$ _____

8. $(x + 7)(2x - 6)$ _____

9. $(4 + 5x)(2 - 3x)$ _____

10. $(5x + 3)(5x + 3)$ _____

11. $(x - 9)(x + 9)$ _____

12. $(2x - 3)(2x - 3)$ _____

13. $(2x - 3)(2x + 3)$ _____

14. $(x + 5)(x + 5)$ _____

15. $(6x + 7)(6x + 1)$ _____

16. $(2x - 3)^2$ _____

17. $(5x + 3)^2$ _____

18. $(x + 5)^2$ _____

19. $(3x - 3)(x + 1)$ _____

20. $(6x - 3)(x + 2)$ _____

21. $(4 - x)(4 + x)$ _____

22. $(7 + 2x)(7 + 2x)$ _____

23. $(4x - 5)(3x + 4)$ _____

24. $(3x - 1)(3x - 2)$ _____

25. $(8x + 3)(7x - 5)$ _____

Solve.

26. $x - 7 - 6x = 13$ _____

27. $2(x - 3) + 9 = 2x + 3$ _____

28. $2(3x + 4) = 2(2x - 8) + 24$ _____

29. $3 - (x - 4) = 8(7 + x)$ _____

30. $\frac{1}{2} + \left(\frac{4}{3}\right)x = \frac{5}{6}$ _____

Factor as the product of linear binomials or write *prime*.

1. $x^2 + 7x + 12$ _____

2. $x^2 + 8x + 12$ _____

3. $x^2 + 13x + 12$ _____

4. $x^2 - 5x + 6$ _____

5. $x^2 - 5x + 4$ _____

6. $x^2 + 6x + 8$ _____

7. $x^2 - 6x + 8$ _____

8. $x^2 + 8x + 16$ _____

9. $x^2 - 8x + 16$ _____

10. $x^2 - 10x + 16$ _____

11. $x^2 + 10x + 24$ _____

12. $x^2 - 11x + 24$ _____

13. $x^2 + 6x + 9$ _____

14. $x^2 - 10x + 25$ _____

15. $x^2 + 2x + 12$ _____

16. $x^2 - 11x + 18$ _____

17. $x^2 - 6x + 7$ _____

18. $x^2 - 2x + 1$ _____

19. $x^2 + 4x + 4$ _____

20. $x^2 - 9x + 20$ _____

Simplify by multiplying binomials and adding common terms.

21. $(2x + 3)(x - 4)$ _____

22. $(2x + 3)(2x - 4)$ _____

23. $(x + 5)^2$ _____

24. $(3x - 2)(3x + 2)$ _____

25. $(3x + 4)^2$ _____

SKILLS PRACTICE 39

For use with Section 5-5
Factoring Quadratic Trinomials—
Third Term Negative

NAME _____

DATE _____

Factor as the product of linear binomials or write *prime*.

1. $x^2 - x - 6$ _____

2. $x^2 + x - 6$ _____

3. $x^2 + 4x - 12$ _____

4. $x^2 + x - 12$ _____

5. $x^2 + 11x - 12$ _____

6. $x^2 - 2x - 24$ _____

7. $x^2 - x - 30$ _____

9. $x^2 + 4x - 45$ _____

9. $x^2 - 4x - 12$ _____

10. $x^2 - x - 2$ _____

11. $x^2 - 3x - 2$ _____

12. $x^2 - 3x - 4$ _____

13. $x^2 + 4x - 5$ _____

14. $x^2 - 6x - 5$ _____

15. $x^2 - 3x - 10$ _____

16. $x^2 - 25$ _____

17. $x^2 - 8x + 12$ _____

18. $x^2 + 9x + 18$ _____

19. $x^2 - 1$ _____

20. $x^2 - 2x + 1$ _____

21. Sam and Charlie found that they averaged the same amount of
time doing each factoring problem. After making this observation,
they found that they each could do 2 problems per minute. If Sam
started 6 minutes before Charlie, how long would they both have
to work before they did a total of 50 problems? Use variables and
expressions.

_____

_____

Name the polynomials by degree and number of terms.

22. $x^2 - 25$ _____

23. $3x^2 - 5x + 9$ _____

24. $7x^3 + 6x^2 + 6x$ _____

25. $x + 7$ _____

SKILLS PRACTICE 40
For use with Section 5-6
Factoring Quadratic Trinomials—
First Coefficient Not 1

NAME _____

DATE _____

Factor as the product of linear binomials or write *prime*.

1. $2x^2 + 5x + 2$ _____

2. $2x^2 + 7x + 3$ _____

3. $2x^2 + x - 3$ _____

4. $2x^2 + 5x - 3$ _____

5. $2x^2 - 7x + 3$ _____

6. $3x^2 - 13x + 4$ _____

7. $3x^2 - 8x + 4$ _____

8. $4x^2 - 4x - 3$ _____

9. $2x^2 - 7x - 15$ _____

10. $25x^2 - 10x - 3$ _____

11. $9x^2 - 1$ _____

12. $4x^2 - 20x + 25$ _____

13. $2x^2 + x + 1$ _____

14. $6x^2 - x - 1$ _____

15. $4x^2 - 5x - 1$ _____

16. $6x^2 + 5x - 6$ _____

17. $3x^2 - 10x + 3$ _____

18. $2x^2 - 3x - 2$ _____

19. $4x^2 - x - 5$ _____

20. $3x^2 + 2x + 1$ _____

Multiply.

21. $(2x + 2)(3x - 2)$ _____

22. $(2x + 1)^2$ _____

23. $(x - 5)(x + 5)$ _____

24. $(x + 9)(2x - 3)$ _____

25. $(x - 1)^2$ _____

SKILLS PRACTICE 41
For use with Section 5-7
Factoring a Difference of Two Squares

NAME _____

DATE _____

Factor as the product of linear binomials or write *prime*.

1. $x^2 - 4$ _____

2. $x^2 - 9$ _____

3. $x^2 - 16$ _____

4. $x^2 - 25$ _____

5. $4x^2 - 1$ _____

6. $9x^2 - 1$ _____

7. $4x^2 - 9$ _____

8. $9x^2 - 49$ _____

9. $1 - 4x^2$ _____

10. $25 - 36x^2$ _____

11. $x^2 - 1$ _____

12. $x^2 + 1$ _____

13. $x^2 - 25$ _____

14. $x^2 + 25$ _____

15. $x^2 - 81$ _____

16. $x^2 - 8$ _____

17. $4 - x^2$ _____

18. $9 - 25x^2$ _____

19. $12 - x^2$ _____

20. $x^2 - y^2$ _____

Factor.

21. $x^2 + 5x + 6$ _____

22. $3x^2 + 4x + 1$ _____

23. $4x^2 - 3x - 1$ _____

24. $x^2 - 4x + 4$ _____

25. $x^2 - 2x + 1$ _____

Square the binomials.

1. $(x + 2)^2$ _____

2. $(x - 3)^2$ _____

3. $(x + 1)^2$ _____

4. $(2x + 1)^2$ _____

5. $(3x - 1)^2$ _____

6. $(5x + 2)^2$ _____

7. $(1 + 3x)^2$ _____

8. $(4x - 1)^2$ _____

9. $(5 - 3x)^2$ _____

10. $(2x - 3)^2$ _____

11. $(2x - 3)^2$ _____

12. $(4x - 5)^2$ _____

13. $(x + y)^2$ _____

14. $(x - 2y)^2$ _____

15. $(3x - y)^2$ _____

16. $(3x + 2y)^2$ _____

17. $(5x + 4)^2$ _____

18. $(4x + 5)^2$ _____

19. $(x - 1)^2$ _____

20. $(1 - x)^2$ _____

Factor if possible. If not, state prime.

21. $x^2 - 1$ _____

22. $x^2 + 1$ _____

23. $x^2 + 3x + 2$ _____

24. $x^2 - 3x - 4$ _____

25. $x^2 - 4x + 5$ _____

Factor as the square of a binomial. If it cannot be written as such, state the reason why.

1. $x^2 + 4x + 4$ _____

2. $x^2 + 2x + 1$ _____

3. $x^2 + 6x + 9$ _____

4. $x^2 - 10x + 25$ _____

5. $x^2 - 12x + 36$ _____

6. $x^2 - 14x + 49$ _____

7. $x^2 - 2x - 1$ _____

8. $x^2 + 16x - 64$ _____

9. $x^2 + 4x + 8$ _____

10. $x^2 - 8x + 16$ _____

11. $x^2 - 4x + 1$ _____

12. $x^2 + 6x - 9$ _____

13. $x^2 - 24x + 144$ _____

14. $x^2 + 50x + 625$ _____

15. $x^2 + 28x + 196$ _____

16. $x^2 + 9x + 81$ _____

17. $x^2 + 1$ _____

18. $x^2 - 30x + 625$ _____

19. $4x^2 + 4x + 1$ _____

20. $9x^2 - 6x + 1$ _____

21. Multiply: $(3x + 1)(2x - 3)$ _____

22. Square: $(2x - 1)^2$ _____

23. Simplify: $2(x^2 - 3x + 4) - (3x^2 - 4x + 5)$ _____

24. Evaluate $|2x - 3|$ if x is

    a. -2 _____

    b. 2 _____

25. Simplify $\dfrac{4x - 6}{4}$. _____

Factor. If the result is the square of a binomial, write it as such. If the result is prime, so state.

1. $x^2 + 7x + 12$ _____

2. $x^2 - 7x + 12$ _____

3. $x^2 - x - 12$ _____

4. $x^2 + 4x - 12$ _____

5. $x^2 - 4x - 12$ _____

6. $5x^2 + 6x + 1$ _____

7. $3x^2 + 2x - 1$ _____

8. $2x^2 + 7x + 3$ _____

9. $2x^2 + 5x + 2$ _____

10. $4x^2 - 8x + 3$ _____

11. $x^2 - 36$ _____

12. $x^2 - 64$ _____

13. $2x^2 + 5x - 12$ _____

14. $x^2 - 8x + 16$ _____

15. $x^2 - 2x + 4$ _____

16. $x^2 + 10x + 25$ _____

17. $x^2 + 2x + 1$ _____

18. $x^2 - 2x + 1$ _____

19. $x^2 - 1$ _____

20. $x^2 + 1$ _____

21. $x^2 + 6x + 9$ _____

22. $x^2 + 10x + 16$ _____

23. $x^2 + 6x - 16$ _____

24. $x^2 + 14x - 49$ _____

25. $x^2 - 5x - 50$ _____

Simplify.

26. $2(x + 3) + 4(x^2 - 5x + 7)$ _____

27. $(2x - 5)(3x + 1)$ _____

28. $(3x + 1)^2$ _____

29. $(0.2)^3$ _____

30. $\frac{3}{4} - \frac{1}{2}\left(\frac{2}{5}\right) + 11\frac{1}{3}$ _____

31. 75% of 18 is _____ .

32. List the factors of 12. _____

SKILLS PRACTICE 45

For use with Section 5-10
Radicals, Irrational Numbers,
and the Closure Axioms

NAME _____

DATE _____

State whether each of the following sets is closed under the given
operation.

1. {even integers}

    a. addition _____   **b.** multiplication _____   **c.** division _____

2. {positive even integers}

    a. addition _____   **b.** subtraction _____

    c. multiplication _____   **d.** division _____

3. {positive multiples of 4}

    a. multiplication _____   **b.** division _____

    c. addition _____   **d.** subtraction _____

4. {non-zero integers}

    a. addition _____   **b.** division _____

5. {positive numbers}

    a. division _____   **b.** subtraction _____

    c. square root _____   **d.** raising to powers _____

6. Write an example of each of the following:

    a. a real number _____   **b.** an integer _____   **c.** an irrational number ____

    d. a negative irrational number _____   **e.** a number which is not real _____

7. Is 3.14 rational or irrational? Use the appropriate definition to
justify your answer.

_____

8. Solve: $2x - (3x + 4) = 7$ _____

9. Evaluate $-x^2$ if x is

    a. -3 _____   **b.** 4 _____

10. Write an example of a trinomial square. _____

11. Write 81 as a power of 3. _____

12. Change $\dfrac{5}{12}$ into a decimal. _____

13. If you start your homework at 7:10 pm and work for 95 minutes,
when do you finish?

_____

SKILLS PRACTICE 46
Chapter 5 Review
Some Operations with Polynomials
and Radicals

NAME _____

DATE _____

1. **a.** Write an example of an expression which is a polynomial.

   _____

   b. Write an example of an expression which is not a polynomial.

   _____

Name the polynomial by degree and number of terms.

2. $x^2 - 3x + 5$ _____

3. $x + 5$ _____

4. x^2 _____

5. $x^3 - 4x^2 + 7x - 9$ _____

Simplify by multiplying and adding common terms.

6. $(x + 3)(x - 2)$ _____

7. $(3x + 1)(2x + 3)$ _____

8. $(4x - 1)^2$ _____

9. $(6x + 1)(6x - 1)$ _____

10. $(3x - 5)(4x + 3)$ _____

11. $(x + 1)^2$ _____

12. $(x - 1)^2$ _____

13. $(x + 1)(x - 1)$ _____

14. $(7x - 2)(x + 4)$ _____

15. $(3x - 2)^2$ _____

Factor. If prime, so state.

16. $x^2 + x - 6$ _____

17. $2x^2 - 7x - 4$ _____

18. $25x^2 - 10x - 3$ _____

19. $x^2 - 5x + 6$ _____

20. $x^2 - 6x + 9$ _____

21. $x^2 + 1$ _____

22. $x^2 - 1$ _____

23. $x^2 - 2x + 1$ _____

24. $x^2 + 2x - 1$ _____

25. $9x^2 - 16$ _____

26. $4x^2 + 4x - 3$ _____

27. $x^2 + 9x - 10$ _____

28. $x^2 - 9x + 10$ _____

29. $6x^2 + x - 1$ _____

30. $4x^2 - 21x + 5$ _____

31. $x^2 + 10x + 25$ _____

32. $x^2 - 25$ _____

33. $x^2 - 4x + 4$ _____

34. $x^2 - 4$ _____

35. $x^2 + x - 2$ _____

36. State whether each of the following numbers are rational, irrational, or neither.

   a. 4 _____

   b. $\sqrt{4}$ _____

   c. 14 _____

   d. $\sqrt{14}$ _____

For use with Section 6-1 and 6-2
Evaluating Radical Expressions

NAME _____

DATE _____

Use a calculator to evaluate. State whether the original number is rational or irrational. Give rational numbers as exact values. Round irrational numbers to 2 decimal places.

1. $\sqrt{36}$ _____

2. $\sqrt{6.25}$ _____

3. $\sqrt{62.5}$ _____

4. $\sqrt{625}$ _____

5. $\sqrt{120}$ _____

6. $\sqrt{289}$ _____

7. $-\sqrt{75}$ _____

8. $-\sqrt{2.89}$ _____

Use a calculator to find a value. Write all decimal places for exact decimals. Write repeating decimals using standard bar notation. If the value is irrational, round the answer to 2 decimal places. Simplify under the radical sign before you take square roots.

9. $\sqrt{25 - 16}$ _____

10. $\sqrt{25} - \sqrt{16}$ _____

11. $\sqrt{(25)(16)}$ _____

12. $(\sqrt{25})(\sqrt{16})$ _____

13. $5 + \sqrt{8}$ _____

14. $\sqrt{8} - 9$ _____

15. $7\sqrt{9}$ _____

16. $5\sqrt{10}$ _____

17. $\dfrac{5 + \sqrt{8}}{7}$ _____

18. $\dfrac{8 + \sqrt{6}}{12}$ _____

19. $\dfrac{12 - \sqrt{8 + 2(3)(7)}}{6}$ _____

20. $\dfrac{14 + \sqrt{5 - 6(7)(8)}}{-9}$ _____

Factor.

21. $x^2 - 4$ _____

22. $x^2 - 4x + 4$ _____

23. $x^2 - x - 2$ _____

24. $2x^2 - 3x - 2$ _____

25. $3x^2 - 5x - 2$ _____

1. Write the definition of $|n|$.

Evaluate the absolute values.

2. $|3|$ _____   **3.** $|-4|$ _____

4. $|x + 5|$ if x is

   a. 8 _____   **b.** -8 _____

5. $|2x - 3|$ if x is

   a. 8 _____   **b.** -8 _____

6. $|5 - x|$ if x is

   a. 8 _____   **b.** -8 _____

Find the values of x which will make the absolute value statements true. Write the solution set.

7. $|x| = 8$ _____   **8.** $|x| = 7$ _____

9. $|x| = -6$ _____   **10.** $|x + 3| = 8$ _____

11. $|x + 5| = 12$ _____   **12.** $|x - 6| = 9$ _____

13. $|x - 6| = -6$ _____   **14.** $|5 - x| = 8$ _____

15. $|8 - x| = 12$ _____   **16.** $|2x - 3| = 5$ _____

17. $|3x + 4| = 10$ _____   **18.** $|6 + 2x| = 6$ _____

19. $|2x + 8| = 8$ _____   **20.** $|2x + 8| = 0$ _____

Factor each polynomial.

21. $x^2 - 7x + 12$ _____

22. $x^2 - 4x - 12$ _____

23. $x^2 - x - 12$ _____

24. $x^2 + 1$ _____

25. $x^2 + 2x + 1$ _____

Find the solution set. Round irrational answers to two decimal places.

1. $x^2 = 64$ _____

2. $x^2 = 28$ _____

3. $x^2 = -9$ _____

4. $(x + 1)^2 = 4$ _____

5. $(x + 2)^2 = 1$ _____

6. $(x + 3)^2 = 16$ _____

7. $(x - 5)^2 = -9$ _____

8. $(x - 4)^2 = 10$ _____

9. $(x + 7)^2 = 64$ _____

10. $(x - 8)^2 = 8$ _____

11. $(x - 1)^2 = 0$ _____

12. $(2x + 1)^2 = 25$ _____

13. $(2x - 1)^2 = 20$ _____

14. $(3x - 4)^2 = 49$ _____

15. $(4x + 1)^2 = 18$ _____

16. $(5x)^2 = 25$ _____

17. $(8x)^2 = 108$ _____

18. $(3 - x)^2 = 100$ _____

19. $(2 - 3x)^2 = 45$ _____

20. $(5x + 2)^2 = -1$ _____

Solve each of the following absolute value equations.

21. $|x| = 25$ _____

22. $|5x| = 25$ _____

23. $|x - 5| = 25$ _____

24. $|5 - x| = 25$ _____

25. $|2x - 5| = -25$ _____

Write the left member as a binomial squared. Solve the equation by taking the square root of both members. Round irrational answers to two decimal places.

1. $x^2 + 2x + 1 = 4$ _____

2. $x^2 + 6x + 9 = 16$ _____

3. $x^2 - 4x + 4 = 49$ _____

4. $x^2 - 10x + 25 = 36$ _____

5. $x^2 - 6x + 9 = 10$ _____

6. $x^2 - 14x + 49 = 49$ _____

7. $x^2 + 20x + 100 = 196$ _____

8. $x^2 + 8x + 16 = 20$ _____

9. $x^2 - 2.2x + 1.21 = 5$ _____

10. $x^2 - 16x + 64 = 130$ _____

11. $x^2 + 9x + 20.25 = 64$ _____

12. $x^2 + 2x + 1 = -4$ _____

13. $x^2 - 4x + 4 = 0$ _____

14. $x^2 + x + .25 = 1$ _____

15. $x^2 - 7x + 12.25 = 40$ _____

16. $x^2 - 6x + 9 = 8$ _____

17. $x^2 - 22x + 121 = 120$ _____

18. $x^2 + 24x + 144 = 144$ _____

19. $x^2 - 12x + 26 = -78$ _____

20. $x^2 + 3x + 2.25 = 6.25$ _____

Solve.

21. $|2x + 3| = 49$ _____

22. $(2x + 3)^2 = 49$ _____

23. $2x + 3 = 49$ _____

24. $2(x + 3) = 49$ _____

25. $8 - (x - 5) = 2(3x - 4)$ _____

SKILLS PRACTICE 51

For use with Section 6-6
Completing the Square

NAME _____

DATE _____

Square the binomial in one step.

1. $(x - 6)^2$ _____

2. $(x + 1)^2$ _____

3. $(x + 3)^2$ _____

4. $(x - 5)^2$ _____

5. $(x + 7)^2$ _____

6. $(x - 2)^2$ _____

Add the number needed to complete the square. Write the result as the square of a binomial.

7. $x^2 + 2x + \cdots$ _____

8. $x^2 - 2x + \cdots$ _____

9. $x^2 - 6x + \cdots$ _____

10. $x^2 + 8x + \cdots$ _____

11. $x^2 - 10x + \cdots$ _____

12. $x^2 + 4x + \cdots$ _____

13. $x^2 + 12x + \cdots$ _____

14. $x^2 + x + \cdots$ _____

15. $x^2 - 14x + \cdots$ _____

16. $x^2 + 9x + \cdots$ _____

17. $x^2 + 36x + \cdots$ _____

18. $x^2 + 16x + \cdots$ _____

19. $x^2 - 64x + \cdots$ _____

20. $x^2 - x + \cdots$ _____

Solve.

21. $x^2 + 6x + 9 = 16$ _____

22. $(x + 5)^2 = 16$ _____

23. $|4 - 5x| = 64$ _____

24. $x^2 - 2x + 1 = -9$ _____

25. $2x - 3 = 25$ _____

SKILLS PRACTICE 52

For use with Section 6-7
Solving Quadratic Equations by
Completing the Square

NAME _____

DATE _____

Solve by completing the square.

1. $x^2 + 6x + 5 = 0$ _____

2. $x^2 - 6x + 8 = 0$ _____

3. $x^2 + 4x + 3 = 0$ _____

4. $x^2 - 8x - 9 = 0$ _____

5. $x^2 - 4x - 5 = 0$ _____

6. $x^2 + 2x - 8 = 0$ _____

7. $x^2 + 2x - 3 = 0$ _____

8. $x^2 + 10x + 10 = 0$ _____

9. $x^2 + 3x - 4 = 0$ _____

10. $x^2 - 5x + 6 = 0$ _____

11. $x^2 - 7x + 12 = 0$ _____

12. $x^2 - x - 2 = 0$ _____

13. $x^2 + 5x - 4 = 0$ _____

14. $x^2 - 9x + 10 = 0$ _____

Solve. Make sure that the coefficient of the quadratic term is 1 by
dividing each term by the coefficient x^2.

15. $2x^2 - 8x + 6 = 0$ _____

16. $3x^2 + 6x + 3 = 0$ _____

17. $4x^2 - 20x + 28 = 0$ _____

18. $3x^2 + 3x + 3 = 0$ _____

19. $5x^2 - 15x - 21 = 0$ _____

20. $4x^2 - 7x + 8 = 0$ _____

Solve.

21. $x^2 = 25$ _____

22. $x^2 - 49 = 0$ _____

23. $|x + 5| = 36$ _____

24. $(x + 5)^2 = 36$ _____

25. $x^2 - 6x + 9 = 64$ _____

52   Foerster *Algebra I*

State the values of a, b, and c that you would place into the quadratic formula.

1. $2x^2 - x + 7 = 0$ _____

2. $x^2 + 5x - 8 = 0$ _____

3. $5x^2 + 6x - 12 = 0$ _____

4. $3x^2 - 9x = 13$ _____

Solve by using the quadratic formula. Write the equation in the form $ax^2 + bx + c = 0$ first.

5. $x^2 + 4x + 3 = 0$ _____

6. $x^2 - 4x + 3 = 0$ _____

7. $x^2 - 5x - 6 = 0$ _____

8. $x^2 - 5x + 6 = 0$ _____

9. $2x^2 + 7x + 3 = 0$ _____

10. $2x^2 + 5x - 12 = 0$ _____

11. $3x^2 + 2x - 1 = 0$ _____

12. $x^2 + 6x + 9 = 0$ _____

13. $x^2 + 10x + 16 = 0$ _____

14. $x^2 + x + 2 = 0$ _____

15. $x^2 - 2x + 1 = 0$ _____

16. $4x^2 + 5x - 8 = 0$ _____

17. $5x^2 - x - 1 = 0$ _____

18. $-x^2 + 2x + 5 = 0$ _____

19. $2x^2 - 3x + 8 = 0$ _____

20. $3x^2 - 5x - 6 = 0$ _____

Solve without the use of the quadratic formula.

21. $x^2 - 6x + 8 = 0$ _____

22. $(x + 5)^2 = 45$ _____

23. $|2x - 5| = 45$ _____

24. $2x - 5 = 45$ _____

25. $x^2 + 4x + 4 = 49$ _____

Each of the following problems uses the formula $d = rt - 5t^2$.
Replace r with the given value for each problem.

1. Adam tossed a baseball into the air with an initial upward velocity of 10 meters per second.
   a. Write an equation relating the distance in meters of the ball above where it was tossed t seconds after it was tossed.
   b. How high above where it was tossed would the ball be after

      i. 1 second _____

      ii. 0.5 seconds _____

      iii. 1.5 seconds _____
   c. When did the ball fall back to the level at which it was tossed?

      _____

   d. The ball reaches its maximum height when t is one-half of how long it took the ball to get back to where it was tossed. When did this happen? How high did the ball go?

   e. Would the ball ever reach a height of 10 meters? Justify your answer with figures.

      _____

2. Kenneth threw a basketball toward the hoop. At the time the ball left his hands it was travelling at a rate of 8 meters per second.
   a. How many meters above his hands was the ball after

      i. 1 second _____

      ii. 0.5 seconds _____

      iii. 1.5 seconds _____
   b. After 0.5 seconds, was the ball on its way up or down? Justify your answer.

      _____

   c. i. How many meters was the ball above his hands after 0.2 seconds?

         _____

      ii. If the ball left Kenneth's hands at a distance of 3 meters above the floor, how far from the floor will the ball be after 0.2 seconds?

         _____

   d. Given that the ball left Kenneth's hands 3 meters above the floor, if Kenneth misses the shot, how long will it take the ball to hit the floor?

      _____

   e. The ceiling of the gym has beams at a height of 15 meters above the floor. Can the ball possibly touch one of these beams? Justify your answer.

      _____

1. The given numbers are discriminants of quadratic equations.
   Put check marks in the appropriate spaces according to what
   the solutions to the equations would be.

Discriminant	real	rational	irrational
45			
−6			
36			
0			
8			

Find the discriminant and state whether the solutions would be real or
not real. If real, state whether they would be rational or irrational.

2. $x^2 - 3x + 4 = 0$ _____

3. $2x^2 - 5x + 2 = 0$ _____

4. $x^2 + 6x - 8 = 0$ _____

5. $3x^2 - x - 1 = 0$ _____

6. $x^2 + 5x + 6 = 0$ _____

7. $x^2 - 7x + 9 = 0$ _____

8. $x^2 + 2x + 3 = 0$ _____

9. $2x^2 + 8x - 7 = 0$ _____

10. $2x^2 - 7x + 3 = 0$ _____

11. $4x^2 - 4x - 3 = 0$ _____

12. $9x^2 - 1 = 0$ _____

13. $6x^2 - x - 1 = 0$ _____

14. $5x^2 + 5x + 5 = 0$ _____

15. $3x^2 - 8x + 4 = 0$ _____

16. $x^2 - 3x - 3 = 0$ _____

17. $x^2 - 8x + 9 = 0$ _____

18. $x^2 = 1$ _____

19. $x^2 - 4x = -4$ _____

20. $2x^2 = -5x - 2$ _____

Solve.

21. $(2x - 5)^2 = 0$ _____

22. $x^2 - 6x + 9 = 0$ _____

23. $3x^2 - 10x + 3 = 0$ _____

24. $3x^2 - 10x + 12 = 0$ _____

25. $3x - 10 = 0$ _____

SKILLS PRACTICE 56
Chapter 6 Review
Quadratic Equations

NAME _____

DATE _____

Solve without the use of the quadratic formula.

1. $|x - 6| = 9$ _____

2. $|4x + 1| = 33$ _____

3. $|7x - 9| = -8$ _____

4. $|8 - x| = 7$ _____

5. $(x + 3)^2 = 25$ _____

6. $(3x - 1)^2 = 64$ _____

7. $x^2 - 4x + 4 = 36$ _____

8. $x^2 + 2x + 1 = 5$ _____

9. $x^2 + 8x - 9 = 0$ _____

10. $x^2 - 5x + 4 = 0$ _____

11. $2x^2 + 8x - 12 = 0$ _____

Solve by using the quadratic formula.

12. $x^2 + 7x + 12 = 0$ _____

13. $2x^2 - 3x + 1 = 0$ _____

14. $3x^2 + 4x - 9 = 0$ _____

15. $6x^2 - 3x + 1 = 0$ _____

16. $x^2 - 8x = -12$ _____

17. Find the discriminant of each of the equations in Problems 12-16 and show that the solutions are indicated by the discriminant.

_____

18. A football was kicked into the air with an initial velocity of 16 meters per second.

   a. Write the equation which relates distance above where the ball was kicked with respect to time.

   _____

   b. After what time(s) was the ball at a height of 12 meters?

   _____

   c. How high was the ball after 2 seconds? Was it on the way up or the way down? Justify your answer.

   _____

   d. How high was the ball after 3 seconds? _____
   e. How many seconds did it take the ball to fall back to the same level from which it was kicked?

   _____

Simplify. Write answers with no grouping symbols.

1. $7(3x - 14)$ _____

2. $(2x - 3)^2$ _____

3. $(x + 4)(2x - 5)$ _____

4. $2x + 7 + 9(7 - 2x)$ _____

5. $\frac{5}{6}y(-12)$ _____

6. $2(x^2 - 3x + 4) - 5(x^2 + 2x - 3)$ _____

7. $\frac{(6x^2 + 9x - 12)}{2}$ _____

8. $6 + \frac{2^3(3)}{6 - 4}$ _____

Evaluate for the given values of the variable.

9. $6x - 23$
  a. $x = -2$ _____   **b.** $x = 12$ _____

10. $\frac{3}{4}x^2$
  a. $x = 5$ _____   **b.** $x = 0.2$ _____

11. $8 - 2(3x - 5)$
  a. $x = 0$ _____   **b.** $x = -\frac{2}{3}$ _____

12. $3y^2 - y - 4$
  a. $y = 2$ _____   **b.** $y = -6$ _____

13. $\frac{|3x + 4|}{7 - x}$
  a. $x = -3$ _____   **b.** $x = 12$ _____

State the axiom, property, or definition which justifies each of the following.

14. $2x + 3 = 3 + 2x$ _____

15. $-x = -1(x)$ _____

16. If $5 = x - 2$, then $x - 2 = 5$. _____

17. $3(x - 12) = 3x - 36$. _____

18. $2(3 \cdot 4) = (2 \cdot 3)4$ _____

Factor.

19. $x^2 - 25$ _____

20. $x^2 - 6x + 8$ _____

21. $x^2 - x - 12$ _____

22. $3x^2 + x - 2$ _____

Solve and check.

23. $x + 3 = 7$ _____

24. $2x - 5 = 18$ _____

25. $0.3 - 2.5x = -0.7$ _____

26. $4x + 3 = 8x - 5$ _____

SKILLS PRACTICE 58
For use with Section 7-1
Evaluating Expressions Containing
Two Variables

NAME _____

DATE _____

Evaluate the given values of the variables.

1. $3x + 2y$ for

    a. $x = 7$ and $y = 2$ _____

    b. $x = -6$ and $y = 4$ _____

    c. $x = 2\frac{2}{3}$ and $y = 2\frac{1}{2}$ _____

    d. $x = 0.4$ and $y = -2.3$ _____

2. $6x - y$ for

    a. $x = 8$ and $y = -3$ _____

    b. $x = -6$ and $y = 4$ _____

    c. $x = 3.4$ and $y = -5.2$ _____

3. $x^2 + 3y$ for

    a. $x = -4$ and $y = 8$ _____

    b. $x = 6$ and $y = -9$ _____

    c. $x = 0.4$ and $y = 0.4$ _____

    d. $x = \frac{1}{2}$ and $y = \frac{5}{12}$ _____

4. $2x^2 - y^2$ for

    a. $x = 3$ and $y = 4$ _____

    b. $x = -2$ and $y = -6$ _____

    c. $x = \frac{1}{3}$ and $y = \frac{2}{3}$ _____

5. $7 - (3x - 5y)$ for

    a. $x = 5$ and $y = 0$ _____

    b. $x = 0$ and $y = 2$ _____

    c. $x = -8$ and $y = 3$ _____

6. $(x + y)^2$ for

    a. $x = 5$ and $y = -9$ _____

    b. $x = -5$ and $y = 9$ _____

7. $x^2 + 2xy + y^2$ for

    a. $x = 5$ and $y = -9$ _____

    b. $x = -5$ and $y = 9$ _____

8. Multiply $(x + 4)^2$. _____

9. Factor $x^2 - 6x - 16$. _____

10. Factor $3x^2 + 7x + 2$. _____

11. Factor $3x^2 - 5x - 2$. _____

12. Solve $x + 3 = 25$. _____

13. Solve $(x + 3)^2 = 25$. _____

Plot each of the following points on a Cartesian coordinate plane.

1. (1, 4) _____   **2.** (−3, 5) _____

3. (8, −3) _____   **4.** (−5, −4) _____

5. (0, 0) _____   **6.** (5, 0) _____

7. (0, 4) _____   **8.** (0, −3) _____

9. (−6, 0) _____

10. Which one(s) of the points listed above is

    a. in the first quadrant _____   **b.** in the second quadrant _____

    c. in the third quadrant _____   **d.** in the fourth quadrant _____

    e. on the origin _____   **f.** on the x axis _____

    g. on the y axis _____

11. a. Plot the points (3, 5) and (−6, −2) on a Cartesian graph.

    _____

    b. Carefully connect the points with a straight line.

    _____

    c. To the nearest 0.1 unit, estimate the point where the line crosses the x-axis.

    _____

    d. To the nearest 0.1 unit, estimate the point where the line crosses the y-axis.

    _____

12. Solve $2 + 3(x - 5) = 3 - (2x + 6)$. _____

13. For the expression $2x^2 - 3x + 1$
    a. Evaluate the expression if x is 4. _____

    b. Find the value(s) of x if the expression is 4. _____

14. Write an example of a quadratic trinomial. _____

15. For the expression $|2x + 3|$
    a. Evaluate the expression if x is 4. _____

    b. Evaluate the expression if x is -4. _____

    c. Find the value(s) of x if the expression is 4. _____

    d. Find the value(s) of x if the expression is -4. _____

SKILLS PRACTICE 60
For use with Section 7-3
Graphs of Equations Containing
Two Variables

NAME _____

DATE _____

Draw a graph of the indicated set of points. Connect the points with a straight line.

1.
x	y
-2	-8
0	-4
1	-2
3	2

2.
x	y
-1	4
0	1
1	-2
3	-8

3. If you read the graphs of Problems 1 and 2 from left to right, how do they differ? Which one would you describe as uphill?

_____

4. How many points do you need to plot before you can graph a line?

_____

For Problems 5-9, solve for y in terms of x. That means, isolate y. (Please do not use decimals for fractional values.)

5. $3x + y = 1$ _____

6. $2x - y = 4$ _____

7. $3x + 4y = 12$ _____

8. $2x - 3y = 9$ _____

9. $x + 2y = 0$ _____

10. Give four ordered pairs which are solutions to the equation $3x + y = 1$.

_____

For each equation in Exercises 11-14

a. Pick four convenient values for x and evaluate y depending on the selected values of x.

_____

b. Plot the ordered pairs of x and y. _____

c. Connect the ordered pairs with a straight line. _____

11. $y = 2x - 4$ _____

12. $y = -3x + 1$ _____

13. $y = -\dfrac{3}{4}x + 12$ (Hint: Use multiples of 4 for values of x.)

_____

14. $y = 2x$ _____

15. For the equation $2x - 3y = 6$, first solve for y in terms of x then graph the line using the procedure described for Problems 11-14.

16. Evaluate $2x - 3y$ for
   a. $x = 6$ and $y = 2$ _____
   b. $x = -3$ and $y = -4$ _____

Calculate the x- and y- intercepts for each of the following lines. Use them to plot the graph of the line.

1. $2x + 3y = 12$ _____

2. $4x - 3y = 12$ _____

3. $5x - y = 5$ _____

4. $x + 3y = 9$ _____

5. $x - y = -5$ _____

6. $\frac{1}{2}x + \frac{1}{3}y = 3$ _____

7. $0.3x - 0.4y = -1.2$ _____

8. $3x + y = -2$ _____

9. For the line $2x - 3y = 3$
   a. Solve for y in terms of x.
   b. Find 3 ordered pairs which are solutions to the equation.

   _____

   c. Use these points to graph the line. _____

   d. Calculate the x- and y-intercepts. _____
   e. Show that the calculated values correspond to points on your line.

   _____

   f. i. The x-intercept corresponds to the point (_____, _____).

   ii. The y-intercept corresponds to the point (_____, _____).

10. For the line $x - 3y = 0$
   a. Calculate the x- and y-intercepts. _____
   b. Why can't this line be graphed using the same procedure as in Problems 1-8?

   _____

   c. Plot the graph of the line using any method. _____

Solve.

11. $3x - (x - 5) = 16$ _____

12. $5x + 3(2x + 4) = 8 - 9x$ _____

13. $|2x - 3| = 16$ _____

14. $(2x - 3)^2 = 25$ _____

15. $x^2 - 5x = -6$ _____

a. Plot the two given points and graph the line containing them.
b. Count the rise and the run between the two points.
c. Write the slope as the ratio of the rise over the run.
d. Use the slope to find a third point on the line.

1. $(-2, 2)$, $(3, 4)$ _____

2. $(-3, -1)$, $(-2, -5)$ _____

3. $(-1, -2)$, $(1, 2)$ _____

4. $(2, 1)$, $(8, -2)$ _____

a. State the slope.
b. State the y-intercept.
c. Plot the line using the slope and y-intercept.

5. $y = \dfrac{3}{2}x + 4$ _____

6. $y = -\dfrac{1}{2}x + 5$ _____

7. $y = -x + 3$ _____

8. $y = -4x - 2$ _____

9. $y = x$ _____

10. $y = 2x - 6$ _____

a. Solve for y in terms of x (isolate y).
b. State the slope and y-intercept.
c. Plot the line using the slope and y-intercept.

11. $2x + 3y = 6$ _____

12. $3x - 4y = -12$ _____

13. $x - y = 6$ _____

14. $x + 2y = 0$ _____

a. State the x- and y-intercepts.
b. Solve for y in terms of x.
c. State the slope.
d. Plot the line using the intercepts and check.

15. $3x - 5y = 15$ _____

16. $x + 2y = -8$ _____

17. $4x - 6y = -24$ _____

18. $x - y = 5$ _____

If $y = mx + b$ where m is the slope and b is the y-intercept of the
line, write an equation of a line with the given slope and y-intercept.

19. slope is $\dfrac{2}{3}$, y-intercept is -5 _____

20. slope is -4, y-intercept is 3 _____

Factor.

21. $x^2 - 3x + 2$ _____

22. $x^2 - 25$ _____

SKILLS PRACTICE 63

For use with Section 7-7
Finding the Intersection of Two Graphs
by Accurate Plotting

NAME _____

DATE _____

For each pair of equations, use either the slope-intercept or the two-intercept method to carefully plot the equations on the same set of axes. Find the coordinates of the point where the two lines intersect.

1. $x + 3y = 9$
  $x - y = 1$ _____

2. $2x - 5y = -10$
  $2x + y = 2$ _____

3. $y = 2x$
  $2x + y = -4$ _____

4. $y = 2x - 9$
  $x + 2y = 2$ _____

5. $3x - y = -9$
  $3x + 2y = 9$ _____

6. $3x + 4y = 12$
  $3x + 4y = -12$ _____

7. Write 32 as a power with 2 as the base.

Write the axiom which justifies each of the following statements.

8. If $x = 2 + 3$ and $2 + 3 = 5$, then $x = 5$. _____

9. If $3 = y - 7$, then $y - 7 = 3$. _____

10. $3 + (4 + 5) = (3 + 4) + 5$ _____

11. $x \cdot 5 = 5x$ _____

SKILLS PRACTICE 64
For use with Section 7-7
Finding the Intersection of Two Graphs by
Accurate Plotting

NAME _____

DATE _____

Solve each of the following systems of equations by substitution. Check
the solution by replacing the ordered pair into both equations.

1. $y = 3x$
$x + y = 8$ _____

2. $x = 4y$
$x - y = -3$ _____

3. $x + 2y = 1$
$x = y + 4$ _____

4. $y = 2x - 3$
$x - y = 5$ _____

5. $3x + y = 9$
$2x - y = 6$ _____

6. $x + y = -5$
$2x + 3y = -7$ _____

7. $3x - y = 1$
$9x - 4y = 10$ _____

8. $x - 5y = 10$
$2x + y = -2$ _____

9. $x - y = 4$
$x + y = 12$ _____

10. $y = 4x - 3$
$y = 2x - 2$ _____

11. For the line $2x - 3y = 12$, the x-intercept is _____, the

y-intercept is _____, and the slope is _____.

12. Find 3 ordered pairs which are solutions to the equation $2x - 3y$
$= 12$.
_____

13. Find the slope of the line connecting the points $(-1, 2)$ and $(3, 5)$.

_____

14. Graph the line $2x - y = 8$ by any method. _____

15. Write an equation for a line with slope of 4 and a y-intercept of -5.

_____

SKILLS PRACTICE 65
For use with Section 7-8
Solving Systems of Equations
by Substitution

NAME _____

DATE _____

Solve each of the following systems of equations by linear combination. Check the solution by placing the ordered pair into both equations.

1. $3x + y = 9$
$2x - y = 6$ _____

2. $x - y = 4$
$x + y = 12$ _____

3. $x - 4y = 0$
$x - y = -3$ _____

4. $2x - y = 3$
$x - y = 5$ _____

5. $x - 5y = 10$
$2x + y = -2$ _____

6. $3x - y = 1$
$9x - 4y = 10$ _____

7. $x + y = -5$
$2x + 3y = -7$ _____

8. $2x - 5y = -10$
$2x + y = 2$ _____

9. $3x + 4y = -4$
$x + 2y = -1$ _____

10. $x + y = 17$
$8x - 5y = -20$ _____

11. $2x + 3y = 4$
$3x + 5y = 7$ _____

12. $2x - 5y = -14$
$6x + 2y = 26$ _____

13. $2x + 7y = 10$
$-5x + 3y = -25$ _____

14. $2x - y = 8$
$5x - y = 11$ _____

15. $3x + 4y = -3.9$
$7x - 2y = 4.5$ _____

16. $3x - 2y = -4$
$6x + 4y = 12$ _____

17. Evaluate $|2x - 5|$ if x is

a. 4 _____

b. -4 _____

18. Evaluate $-x^2 + 3$ if x is

a. 4 _____

b. -4 _____

19. Multiply $(2x - 3)^2$. _____

20. Simplify $3 - [5 + 3(x - 2)]$. _____

21. Subtract $12\frac{5}{6}$ from $15\frac{1}{2}$. _____

Set up expressions for each of the problem.
Use those expressions by either evaluating or setting up equations and solving in order to answer the questions.

1. When Roger was a child, he would go to the malls and play on the escalators. His favorite was the escalator going up. When he walked up it, his rate was his rate of stair climbing plus the rate of the escalator. When he started at the top of the up escalator and tried to walk down, his rate was his rate of stair climbing minus the rate of the escalator.

   Let r be Roger's rate of stair climbing and let e be the rate of the escalator.

   a. Write two expressions, one for his rate while walking up the escalator and another for his rate while going down the up escalator.

      _____

   b. If Roger travelled at 1 ft per second while walking down the escalator and 6 feet per second while walking up, find his rate of stair climbing and the rate of the escalator.

      _____

   c. Convert 6 feet per second to miles per hour to give yourself an idea of how fast he was actually moving.

      _____

   d. How fast would Roger have to climb stairs in order for him to appear to stand still on the escalator?

      _____

Graph the lines.

2. $2x - 3y = 6$ _____

3. $x - y = 0$ _____

4. $y = -\dfrac{3}{4}x + 5$ _____

5. Write $4 \cdot x \cdot x \cdot x$ as a power. _____

6. Evaluate $5x^4$ if x is 2. _____

SKILLS PRACTICE 67
Review Chapter 7
Expressions and Equations Containing
Two Variables

NAME _____

DATE _____

For each of the following systems of equations:

a. solve by graphing.
b. solve by substitution.
c. solve by linear combination (addition-subtraction method).

1. $2x - y = -3$
$3x + y = -2$ _____

2. $x + 3y = 6$
$2x - 3y = 3$ _____

2. $5x - 2y = -10$
$x + 2y = -2$ _____

4. $y = 3x + 8$

$y = -\frac{2}{3}x - 3$ _____

5. $3x - 2y = -6$
$x + y = 3$ _____

Simplify.

6. $2x - (3x - 5) + (x + 1)^2$ _____

7. $3x^2 - 2x + 7 - x^2 + 3x + 5$ _____

8. $\dfrac{4x - 6}{3}$ _____

9. Evaluate $\left(\frac{2}{3}\right)x - \left(\frac{1}{2}\right)y$ if
    a. x is 6 and y is 4 _____   **b.** x is 4 and y is -5 _____

10. For the 2 integers 12 and 18,
    a. What is the greatest common factor? _____

    b. What is the least common multiple? _____

State the domain and range of the linear function.

1.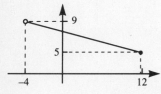

2.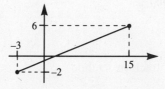

3.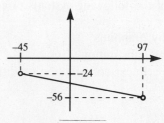

Domain: _____ , Range: _____   Domain: _____ , Range: _____   Domain: _____ , Range: _____

Sketch a graph of the linear function described.

4. Domain: $-3 \le x \le 4$,
Range: $1 \le y \le 6$

5. Domain: $-3 \le x \le 0$,
Range: $2 \le y \le 8$

6. Domain: $-19 < x < 25$,
Range: $-30 < y < -20$

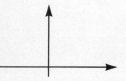

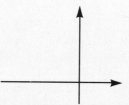

7. ***Washing Machine Problem*** Bill Houseman recently bought a new washing machine. He figures that water and detergent cost him $1.25 per laundry load, plus a fixed monthly cost of $40 for washing machine payments.

   a. Write an equation expressing the total monthly cost in terms of the number of loads washed that month.

   b. How much would it cost Bill if he washes 13 loads a month?

   c. Bill wishes to spend no more than $60 a month, total, for clothes-washing expenses. How many loads can he wash per month?

   d. Sketch the graph of this linear function. Show clearly the domain and range.

8. ***Shampoo Problem*** A 20-ounce container of shampoo costs $3.77, while a 14-ounce container costs only $2.69. Assume that the cost of a container of shampoo is a linear function of the number of ounces in the container.

   a. Define variables for the number of ounces and the number of dollars. Write the given information as ordered pairs.

   b. Find the slope of this linear function.

   c. Use the point-slope form to write an equation for this function.

   d. How would you find out what the manufacturer assumes to be the fixed cost of the container and packaging? What is this fixed cost?

For Problems 1 and 2, calculate x_{av} and y_{av}. Then draw the best-fitting line through the data points and write its equation.

1.

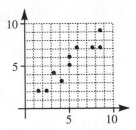

2.

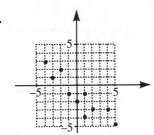

For Problems 3 and 4,

    a. Make a scatter plot of the data.

    b. Find x_{av} and y_{av}, and graph the linear function you think best fits the data.

    c. Write an equation for the linear function you graphed in Part **b.**

    d. Use a graphing calculator to find the equation of the linear function that actually fits the data best.

3.

x	y	x	y
1	−2	6	1
2	−2	7	3
3	0	8	2
4	−1	9	3
4	1	10	6

4.

x	y	x	y	x	y	x	y
1	11	5	7	11	6	14	2
2	9	7	7	11	7	15	4
3	9	7	9	11	4	16	2
4	8	8	8	12	4	17	1
4	10	10	5	12	5	17	3

5. ***Push-up Problem*** You decide to examine the effects of a regular exercise routine on an adult's ability to do push-ups. From observations at the local fitness center you collect the following data for the number of push-ups done, y, after x weeks of training.

x	y	x	y	x	y	x	y
0	6	2	7	4	8	6	9
0	3	2	8	4	10	8	10
1	5	3	6	5	9	8	12
1	6	3	8	6	8	9	11
1	5	4	9	6	10	9	12

    a. Make a scatter plot of the data. Does the data seem to be linearly related?

    b. Find x_{av} and y_{av}, and graph the linear function you think best fits the data.

    c. Write an equation for the linear function you graphed in Part **b.**

    d. Based on your equation, find out, on the average, how many push-ups an adult would be expected to do after 7 weeks of training.

1. Tell the probability for each of the following random experiments:

   a. Choose an odd number from $\{1, 2, 3, 4, 7, 10, 11, 16, 19\}$.   _____

   b. Choose a two-digit number from $\{7, 8, 10, 13, 15, 23\}$.   _____

   c. Choose an even prime number from $\{1, 2, 4, 5, 11, 15, 19, 22\}$.   _____

   d. Choose an outcome in an event space with 120 elements if the sample space has 150 elements.   _____

   e. Choose an outcome in an event space with 30 elements if the sample space has 30 elements.   _____

2. *Number Line Problem* The diagram below shows the integers -6 through 6 on a number line.

If an integer is selected at random from these, find the probability that:

a. it is -3. _____   **b.** it is odd. _____   **c.** it has 2 digits. _____

d. it is positive. _____   **e.** it is at most -1. _____   **f.** it is at least 2. _____

g. it is nonnegative. _____   **h.** it is evenly divisible by 3. ___   **i.** it is evenly divisible by 5. ___

3. *Rectangular Array Problem* The diagram shows ordered pairs (x, y) with integer coordinates. The values of x are from 2 through 7 and the values of y are from -3 through 3.

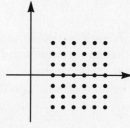

An ordered pair (x, y) is selected at random. What is the probability that:

a. $x > 4$ _____   **b.** $y \le 1$ _____   **c.** $x > 4$ and $y \le 1$ _____

d. $x - y = 2$ _____   **e.** $x + y \ge 5$ _____   **f.** $xy \le 6$ _____

g. $x = 2$ and $y = 0$ _____   **h.** $x = 2$ or $y = 0$ _____   **i.** $xy > 21$ _____

1. Draw a single card at random from a standard 52-card deck. Find the theoretical probability that it is:

   a. a queen _____   **b.** a red 5 _____   **c.** red _____

   d. the 8 of clubs _____   **e.** a 6 or 7 _____   **f.** a black jack _____

   g. the king of hearts _____   **h.** a red face card _____   **i.** a black 4 or a red 5 _____

2. *Dice Roll Experiment* If you roll a pair of dice there are 36 equally likely outcomes.

   a. Write an ordered pair for each possible outcome. For instance, (2, 1) would represent 2 on the first die and 1 on the second die. _____

   b. In how many outcomes are the first die and the second die the same? _____

   c. What is the probability that the first die and the second die are the same? _____

   d. What is the probability that the sum of the two dice equals 10? _____

   e. What is the probability that the sum equals 9 or less? _____

   f. What is the probability that at least one number is even? _____

3. If a couple has four children, there are 16 possible outcomes. For instance, BGBB would represent a boy on the first birth, followed by a girl and then two boys.

   a. List all 16 of the possible outcomes. _____

   b. What is the probability of exactly two girls? _____

   c. What is the probability of at least two boys? _____

   d. What is the probability of at most 1 girl? _____

   e. What is the probability of the oldest child being a girl and the youngest being a boy? _____

SKILLS PRACTICE 72
Chapter 8 Review
Linear Functions, Scattered Data,
and Probability

NAME _____

DATE _____

1. If $y = -0.6x + 44$,

  a. Find y when $x = 15$ _____   **b.** Find x when $y = 43.1$ _____

Sketch a graph of the linear function described.

2. Domain: $-1 < x < 4$, range: $-2 < y < 3$ **3.** slope negative, y-intercept positive

4. The development office at a private women's college wishes to
determine whether there is any relationship between the amount of
money an alumna contributes, y, and the number of years since the
alumna graduated, x. The alumnae office supplied the following
data:

x	y (\$)	x	y (\$)	x	y (\$)	x	y (\$)
1	15	10	80	18	175	25	250
3	30	10	100	20	150	27	300
5	50	12	100	20	200	30	300
8	70	15	140	22	180	32	375
8	60	17	150	25	210	35	400

  a. Make a scatter plot of the data.
  b. Find x_{av} and y_{av} and graph the linear function you think best fits
  the data.
  c. Write an equation for the linear function you graphed in Part **b**.
  d. On the average, how much money would an alumna contribute
  27 years after graduating?

5. *Counting Problem* The names of 30 members of a club are placed
in a hat.
  a. How many different ways could a president be chosen?   _____
  b. How many different ways could a president and then a vice
  president be chosen?   _____
  c. How many different ways could a president, a vice president,
  and then a secretary be chosen?   _____
  d. If Ann, José, and Jamal are members of the club, what is the
  probability that Ann is chosen president, José is chosen vice
  president, and Jamal is chosen secretary?   _____

1. Write the primes from 2 to 37. _____

Write as a product of primes.

2. 18 _____   **3.** 24 _____

4. 48 _____   **5.** 75 _____

6. 120 _____   **7.** 280 _____

8. 325 _____   **9.** 132 _____

10. 625 _____   **11.** 243 _____

12. 343 _____   **13.** 765 _____

14. 1000 _____   **15.** 1989 _____

16. 1521 _____   **17.** 3971 _____

18. 9000 _____   **19.** 2146 _____

20. 40320 _____

21. Change one-fourth mile per minute into miles per hour.

_____

22. If you start a task at 11:36 a.m. and finish 2 and $\frac{1}{2}$ hours later, when did you finish?

_____

23. Change $\frac{44}{3}$ into a mixed number. _____

24. Subtract $11\frac{5}{6}$ from $9\frac{3}{4}$. _____

25. Use a graph to find the slope of the line connecting the points $(3, -4)$ and $(-8, 6)$.

_____

Write the expressions as powers.

1. $x \cdot x \cdot x \cdot x \cdot y \cdot y$ _____

2. $4 \cdot x \cdot x \cdot x$ _____

3. $2 \cdot x \cdot 2 \cdot x \cdot 2 \cdot x$ _____

4. $(xy)(xy)(xy)(xy)$ _____

5. $x^2 \cdot x^2 \cdot x^2 \cdot x^2$ _____

Evaluate the powers for the given values of the variable.

6. x^4 if x is 2 _____

7. $x^4 \cdot y^3$ if x is 2 and y is -3 _____

8. $2x^3$ if x is 4 _____

9. $(2x)^3$ if x is 4 _____

10. $x^3 \cdot x^2$ if x is 2 _____

11. x^5 if x is 2 _____

12. $(x^3)^2$ if x is 2 _____

13. x^6 if x is 2 _____

Write the expression as a single power of x.

14. $x^3 \cdot x^2$ _____

15. $x^4 \cdot x^3$ _____

16. $(x^3)^2$ _____

17. $(x^5)^2$ _____

Write the expression without parentheses.

18. $(xy)^2$ _____

19. $(x \cdot y^2)^3$ _____

20. $(2x)^3$ _____

21. $(xy^2)^3$ _____

22. Simplify $(x + 2y)^2$. _____

23. Simplify $(2x^2 + 3x - 4) - (5x^2 - 8x + 9)$. _____

24. Simplify $\dfrac{4x + 8}{6}$. _____

25. Solve $x - y = 4$
$x + y = 12$. _____

26. Find the slope of the line $3x - 2y = -8$. _____

SKILLS PRACTICE 75

For use with Section 9-3
Exponents, Products, and Powers

NAME _____

DATE _____

1. Using x, a, and b, state the rule for "PRODUCT OF TWO POWERS WITH EQUAL BASES." _____

2. Using x, a, and b, state the rule for "POWER OF A POWER."

_____

3. Using x, y, and a, state the rule for "POWER OF A PRODUCT." _____

Simplify by using the rules stated above.

4. $x^2 \cdot x^3$ _____   5. $x^3 \cdot x^4$ _____

6. $(x^2)^3$ _____   7. $(x^3)^4$ _____

8. $4x^2 \cdot x^3$ _____   9. $4x^3 \cdot 3x^4$ _____

10. $x^6 \cdot x$ _____   11. $5x \cdot x^4$ _____

12. $2x^3 \cdot 5x^8$ _____   13. $6x^4 \cdot y^2 \cdot x^3$ _____

14. $(2x)^3$ _____   15. $(x \cdot y)^3$ _____

16. $(xy)^3$ _____   17. $(x^2 \cdot y^3)^4$ _____

18. $(-2x^2)^3$ _____   19. $(3x^2)^3$ _____

20. $(-5x)(2x^3)$ _____   21. $(x^5)^2 \cdot 5x$ _____

22. $(4^2 \cdot x^3)^2$ _____   23. $(x^3)(x^5)$ _____

24. $(x^3)^5$ _____   25. $(3x)^5$ _____

26. $(2x)(3x^2)(4x^3)$ _____   27. $(8x)^2(-9x)$ _____

28. $x^2 + x^3$ _____   29. $x^2 + x^2$ _____

30. $5x^3 - x^3$ _____

31. Evaluate $\dfrac{3x - 6}{x + 2}$ if x is **a.** -2 _____   **b.** 2 _____

Solve.

32. $7x + 5 = -9$ _____   33. $5(x - 3) = 2x + 3(x - 5)$ _____

34. $x - (x - 5) = 2x - 5$ _____   35. $x^2 + 4x + 3 = 0$ _____

Simplify.

1. $\dfrac{x^6}{x^2}$ _____

2. $\dfrac{x^9}{x^3}$ _____

3. $\dfrac{4^5}{4^3}$ _____

4. $\dfrac{2^4}{-2}$ _____

5. $\dfrac{6y^4}{y}$ _____

6. $\dfrac{12x^6}{x^3}$ _____

7. $\dfrac{6y^4}{3y^3}$ _____

8. $\dfrac{12x^6}{3x^3}$ _____

9. $\dfrac{-24x^3}{4x}$ _____

10. $\dfrac{18x^6}{2x^3}$ _____

11. $\dfrac{12x^6y^8}{4x^3y^4}$ _____

12. $\dfrac{-24x^8y}{6xy}$ _____

13. $\left(\dfrac{x^5}{y^7}\right)\left(\dfrac{y^7}{x^4}\right)$ _____

14. $\left(\dfrac{x^5}{y}\right)\left(\dfrac{y^3}{x^3}\right)$ _____

15. $\left(\dfrac{x^3}{y^2}\right)^4\left(\dfrac{y^{12}}{x}\right)$ _____

16. $\left(\dfrac{y^2}{x^5}\right)^5\left(\dfrac{x^{21}}{y^3}\right)$ _____

17. $\left(\dfrac{2x^3}{2x^5}\right)^4$ _____

18. $\left(\dfrac{x^5 \cdot 2y^3}{y^5 \cdot 3x^2}\right)^2$ _____

19. $\dfrac{x^{10}y^{12}}{(x^2y)^3}$ _____

20. $\dfrac{(x^2y^3)^4}{(xy^2)^3}$ _____

21. $4x^2 - x^2$ _____

22. $(3x^2y)^3$ _____

23. $x^4 + x^5$ _____

24. x^3y^2 _____

25. $2x^4 \cdot 3x^4$ _____

Write fractions equivalent to the given powers.

1. 2^{-3} _____

2. 3^{-2} _____

3. $(-2)^{-4}$ _____

4. $(-5)^{-3}$ _____

5. $\left(\dfrac{2}{3}\right)^{-2}$ _____

6. What integer is equivalent to $\left(\dfrac{1}{8}\right)^{-1}$? _____

7. Evaluate each of the following.

    a. 5^1 _____

    b. -5^{-1} _____

    c. 5^0 _____

Simplify. Write with no powers of variables in the denominator. Leave all numerical coefficients as integers or fractions.

8. $\dfrac{x^4}{x^7}$ _____

9. $\dfrac{y}{y^9}$ _____

10. $x^7 \cdot x^{-9}$ _____

11. $x^{-3} \cdot x^{-2}$ _____

12. $(x^{-2})^{-2}$ _____

13. $(2x)^{-3}$ _____

14. $\dfrac{x^3 y^5}{x^{-4} y^{-2}}$ _____

15. $\dfrac{4x^{-3}}{2x^3}$ _____

16. $\dfrac{x}{x^7}$ _____

17. $\dfrac{y^0}{y^{-7}}$ _____

18. $\dfrac{x^{-2}}{y}$ _____

19. $\dfrac{3^{-2}}{x}$ _____

20. $\dfrac{x^{-4}}{y^{-3}}$ _____

21. $\dfrac{-4y^{-2}}{8x^{-2}}$ _____

Simplify.

22. $(2x^3)^2$ _____

23. $2x^3 \cdot 3x^2$ _____

24. $3x^2(5x - 4)$ _____

25. $(3x + 2)(4x - 1)$ _____

26. $(x^2 + 4x - 5) - (3x^2 - 6x + 4)$ _____

SKILLS PRACTICE 78
For use with Section 9-6
Powers of 10 and Scientific Notation

NAME _____

DATE _____

Write in scientific notation.

1. 213 _____

2. 0.0123 _____

3. 65 thousand _____

4. 90.8×10^{-4} _____

5. 0.00005×10^3 _____

Write in standard notation.

6. 8.9×10^4 _____

7. -7.38×10^{-3} _____

8. 4.5×10^0 _____

9. 2.4567×10^{-5} _____

10. 0.00123×10^3 _____

Find the product or quotient by using the laws of exponents. Do not use a calculator. Express answers in scientific notation.

11. $(2 \times 10^3)(3 \times 10^2)$ _____

12. $(3 \times 10^4)(3 \times 10^{-3})$ _____

13. $(4 \times 10^5)(5 \times 10^{-4})$ _____

14. $(6 \times 10^{-2})(7 \times 10^{-5})$ _____

15. $\dfrac{8 \times 10^8}{2 \times 10^2}$ _____

16. $\dfrac{6 \times 10^{-2}}{3 \times 10^{-5}}$ _____

17. $\dfrac{4 \times 10^3}{5 \times 10^5}$ _____

18. $\dfrac{3 \times 10^{-3}}{4 \times 10^8}$ _____

Use a calculator to find the product or quotient. Express answers in scientific notation.

19. $(3.45 \times 10^3)(2.85 \times 10^8)$ _____

20. $(9.45 \times 10^{-7})(9.74 \times 10^4)$ _____

21. $\dfrac{3.45 \times 10^3}{2.85 \times 10^8}$ _____

22. $\dfrac{9.45 \times 10^{-7}}{9.74 \times 10^{-4}}$ _____

Simplify.

23. $(3x^2)^2$ _____

24. $x^4 x^3$ _____

25. $(x^2 y^3)^4$ _____

26. $\dfrac{4x^5}{6x^{-2}}$ _____

27. $x^2 - (x + 2)(x - 3)$ _____

SKILLS PRACTICE 79
For use with Section 9-7
Problems Involving Numbers
in Scientific Notation

NAME _____

DATE _____

The following problems involve numbers which are either very large
or very small. Use the exponents to make the work easier. Write all
answers in scientific notation.

1. The average high school student sits in a classroom about 6 hours
   a day, 172 days a year. After one year, about how many seconds
   has the average high school student spent in a classroom?

   _____

2. Americans average about 3.5 hours of T.V. viewing per day.
   a. At this rate, after 16 years, how many hours of T.V. would you
      have viewed? _____

   b. How many hours are in a year? _____
   c. The answer you got in part "a" is equivalent to how many
      years?
      _____

3. If light travels at approximately 3×10^5 km/sec, what is its rate in
   cm/sec?

   _____

4. Suppose your grandfather was given a new clock at the time he
   was born. The clock ticked once every second while your
   grandfather was alive, never missing a second. If the clock stopped
   ticking when your grandfather died on his 90th birthday, about
   how many ticks did the clock make while it worked?

   _____

5. The formula for the conversion of mass into energy is $E = mc^2$
   where

   E = energy in ergs
   m = mass in grams
   c = velocity of light in cm/sec (3×10^{10} cm/sec)
   If 1 erg = 2.4×10^{-8} cal., how many calories would you get if
   you converted 3.2 kg. into energy?

   _____

Simplify.

6. $2x^2 + 3x^2$ _____

7. $2x^2 \cdot 3x^2$ _____

8. $(3x^2y^3)^4$ _____

9. $\dfrac{36x^5y^7}{4x^3y^9}$ _____

10. $(x + 2y)^2$ _____

Simplify. Leave no powers of variables in the denominator. Evaluate all powers of numbers. Do not use decimals. If the expression cannot be simplified, so state.

1. x^2x^3 _____

2. $(x^2)^3$ _____

3. $\dfrac{x^2}{x^3}$ _____

4. $x^2 + x^3$ _____

5. $2x^4 \cdot 3x^3$ _____

6. $(2x)^3$ _____

7. $(x^3y^{-3})^5$ _____

8. $\dfrac{8x^6}{2x^4}$ _____

9. 3^{-2} _____

10. $(6x^{-2})(-3x^4)$ _____

11. $(2x^2y^3)^3$ _____

12. $\left(\dfrac{x^3}{y^2}\right)^4$ _____

13. $\left(\dfrac{2x^{-3}}{y^3}\right)^{-2}$ _____

14. $\dfrac{x^4y}{xy}$ _____

15. $4x^3 \cdot 2x^3$ _____

16. $4x^3 - 2x^3$ _____

17. $(x^2y^{-4})^5$ _____

18. $(-2x^4)^3$ _____

19. $\dfrac{x^{-3}y^4}{x^5y^{-2}}$ _____

20. $(5xy^8)^0$ _____

Write in scientific notation.

21. 30405 _____

22. 0.00091 _____

23. 89.5×103 _____

Write in standard notation.

24. 7.8×10^{-3} _____

25. 7.8×10^3 _____

Express the product or quotient in scientific notation.

26. $(2 \times 10^3)(4 \times 10^{-2})$ _____

27. $\dfrac{4 \times 10^{-2}}{2 \times 10^3}$ _____

Multiply the binomials.

1. $(x + 3)(x + 2)$ _____

2. $(2x + 3)(x - 4)$ _____

3. $(3x - 1)(3x + 1)$ _____

4. $(2x + 5)^2$ _____

5. $(3x + 4)(2x - 5)$ _____

Factor as the product of binomials.

6. $x^2 - 5x + 6$ _____

7. $x^2 - x - 6$ _____

8. $x^2 + 6x + 9$ _____

9. $2x^2 - x - 6$ _____

10. $4x^2 + 4x - 3$ _____

Find the greatest common factor.

11. 8, 12 _____

12. 12, 18 _____

13. 24, 60 _____

14. 28, 140 _____

15. 36, 450 _____

Find the greatest common factor.

16. x^2 and x^7 _____

17. x^2y^3 and x^3 _____

18. $4x^5$ and $8x^3$ _____

19. $6x^3$ and $8x$ _____

20. $12x^2y^5$ and $18x^6y^5z$ _____

Find the greatest common factor on each term in the expression.

21. $3x^2 + x^5$ _____

22. $6x^7 + 8x^5$ _____

23. $4x^3 - 4x$ _____

24. $4x^3y - 16x^4y^3$ _____

25. a. Solve the equation $4x - y = 8$ for y in terms of x. _____

   b. What is the slope of this line? _____

   c. What is the y-intercept of this line? _____

26. Solve the system of equations $\quad y = 2x - 9$
$\qquad\qquad\qquad\qquad\qquad x + 2y = 2$ _____

27. Find the slope of the line connecting the points (1, 2) and (3, −4).

_____

28. Find 3 solutions of the equation $2x + 3y = 6$. _____

29. Simplify $\dfrac{4x + 18}{2}$. _____

SKILLS PRACTICE 82
For use with Section 10-3
Factoring Polynomials That
Have Common Factors

NAME _____

DATE _____

Factor completely by first factoring out the greatest common factor and
then factoring the resulting polynomial.

1. $3x^2 + 6x + 3$ _____

2. $5x^2 - 20x + 20$ _____

3. $6x^2 - 6$ _____

4. $9x^2 - 81$ _____

5. $4x^2 - 4x - 48$ _____

6. $4x^2 + 10x + 4$ _____

7. $6x^2 + 4x - 2$ _____

8. $15x^2 + 18x + 3$ _____

9. $2x^2 - 14x + 24$ _____

10. $8x^2 + 20x - 48$ _____

11. $12x^2 + 42x + 18$ _____

12. $12x^2 - 24x + 9$ _____

13. $5x^2 - 20x - 60$ _____

14. $7x^2 + 42x + 63$ _____

15. $5x^2 - 25x - 250$ _____

16. $8x^2 + 8$ _____

17. $x^3 - 64x$ _____

18. $x^4 - 2x^3 + x^2$ _____

19. $5x^2y^2 - 35xy^2 + 60y^2$ _____

20. $x^4 - x^2y^2$ _____

Simplify.

21. $(3x^2)^3$ _____

22. $6x^4 - x^4$ _____

23. $4 - (2 - 8x)$ _____

24. $(3x - 1)^2$ _____

25. $5x^54x^4$ _____

Factor completely by factoring out the common binomial expression first.

1. $(x + 2)y + (x + 2)z$ _____

2. $3(x - 3) + x(x - 3)$ _____

3. $x(2x + 1) + 8(2x + 1)$ _____

4. $y(y - 4) + (y - 4)$ _____

5. $x(2x + 3) + (2x + 3)$ _____

6. $x(4 - x) - (4 - x)$ _____

7. $8x(5x - 1) - (5x - 1)$ _____

8. $4x(x - 2) - 2(x - 2)$ _____

9. $5x(4x - 2) - 6(4x - 2)$ _____

10. $(9x + 2) + 9x(9x + 2)$ _____

11. $x^2(x - 5) - 25(x - 5)$ _____

12. $9x^2(3x - 1) - (3x - 1)$ _____

13. $x^2(x - 4) - 4(x - 4)$ _____

14. $x^2(x^2 - 4) - 9(x^2 - 4)$ _____

15. $x^2(3x + 1) - 9y^2(3x + 1)$ _____

16. $(2x + 1)(x - 2) + 8(x - 2)$ _____

17. $(3x - 1)(3x - 1) + 5(3x - 1)$ _____

18. $(x - 2)(x - 2) - (x - 2)$ _____

19. $(x^2 - 5x)(x - 3) + 6(x - 3)$ _____

20. $(x^2 + 2x)(2x + 1) - (x + 2)(2x + 1)$ _____

Factor completely, then state the Greatest Common Factor.

21. $x^2 - 9, x^2 - 6x + 9$ _____

22. $x^2 - 1, x^2 - 2x + 1$ _____

23. $3x + 9, x^2 - 9$ _____

24. State the least common multiple of 18 and 12. _____

25. State the greatest common factor of 18 and 12. _____

26. Three-fourths of 16 is _____?

27. 45% of 80 is _____?

28. $12\frac{1}{2} \times 4\frac{2}{3} =$ _____?

Factor completely by grouping and then factoring.

1. $x^2 + ax + bx + ab$ _____

2. $x^2 + 2x + xy + 2y$ _____

3. $2x^2 + ax + 2bx + ab$ _____

4. $6x^2 + 2ax + 3bx + ab$ _____

5. $x^2 - 3x + xy - 3y$ _____

6. $6x^2 - 9x + 2xy - 3y$ _____

7. $6x^2 - 3x - 2xy + y$ _____

8. $x^2 - xy - xz + yz$ _____

9. $2x^2 - x - 10xz + 5z$ _____

10. $5x^2 - 3x - 20xy + 12y$ _____

11. $x^3 + 3x^2 - 4x - 12$ _____

12. $2x^3 + 3x^2 - 2x - 3$ _____

13. $x^3 + 3x^2 - 9x - 27$ _____

14. $x^4 - x^2 + 2x^2 - 2$ _____

15. $x^3 + 3x^2 + 5x + 15$ _____

16. $x^3 - 2x^2 - x + 2$ _____

17. $x^3 - 2x^2 + x - 2$ _____

18. $30x^2 + 6x + 35x + 7$ _____

19. $8x^2 + 2x - 12x - 3$ _____

20. $15x^2 - 6x - 20x + 8$ _____

Solve.

21. $2x + 3 = 25$ _____

22. $|2x + 3| = 25$ _____

23. $(2x + 3)^2 = 25$ _____

24. $4x^2 + 12x - 16 = 0$ _____

25. $x^2 - x + 7 = 3$ _____

SKILLS PRACTICE 85

For use with Section 10-6
Factoring Harder Quadratic Trinomials

NAME _____

DATE _____

Use the technique of splitting the middle term to either factor the
polynomial or show that it is prime.

1. $30x^2 + 23x + 3$ _____

2. $24x^2 + 38x + 15$ _____

3. $6x^2 - 29x + 28$ _____

4. $6x^2 - 31x + 40$ _____

5. $6x^2 - 25x + 14$ _____

6. $5x^2 - 4x - 7$ _____

7. $6x^2 + x - 15$ _____

8. $6x^2 - 13x - 5$ _____

9. $6x^2 + 5x - 6$ _____

10. $6x^2 - 5x + 6$ _____

Factor by inspection or splitting the middle term.

11. $6x^2 + 11x + 3$ _____

12. $6x^2 + 11x - 10$ _____

13. $4x^2 + 4x - 15$ _____

14. $6x^2 - 17x - 14$ _____

15. $10x^2 - 9x - 9$ _____

Factor completely by factoring out the Greatest Common Factor first.

16. $8x^2 - 8x - 30$ _____

17. $24x^2 - 28x - 20$ _____

18. $3x^4 - 18x^3 + 27x^2$ _____

19. $18x^3 - 24x^2 - 10x$ _____

20. $25x^2 + 25$ _____

Factor completely using any method.

21. $9x^2 - 81$ _____

22. $x^3 - 6x^2 + x - 6$ _____

23. $x^3 + 2x^2 - 4x - 8$ _____

24. $(x + 3)(x^2) - (x + 3)$ _____

25. $3x^3 - 5x^2 + 3x - 5$ _____

Solve the equations by using the converse of the multiplication property of zero.

1. $(x + 2)(2x + 5) = 0$ _____

2. $(2x - 3)(5x + 1) = 0$ _____

3. $(2x + 1)(x - 6) = 0$ _____

4. $(8x + 1)(7x - 3) = 0$ _____

5. $(x - 2)(x + 4)(x + 5) = 0$ _____

6. $(2x + 3)(4x - 1)(5x + 3) = 0$ _____

Factor then solve by using the converse of the multiplication property of zero.

7. $x^2 - 5x + 6 = 0$ _____

8. $x^2 - x - 6 = 0$ _____

9. $2x^2 - 3x + 1 = 0$ _____

10. $4x^2 - 1 = 0$ _____

11. $2x^2 - 5x + 3 = 0$ _____

12. $6x^2 + 7x - 3 = 0$ _____

13. $x^2 - 7x + 12 = 0$ _____

Solve by factoring or use the quadratic formula. Make sure the polynomial is equal to 0 before you factor or use the formula.

14. $4x^2 - 12x + 5 = 0$ _____

15. $x^2 - x = 2$ _____

16. $x^2 = 9$ _____

17. $x^2 + 5x - 5 = 0$ _____

18. $x^2 - 8 = 0$ _____

19. $2x^2 + 7x = -6$ _____

20. $3x^2 + 5 = 8x$ _____

Factor completely.

21. $8x^2 - 8$ _____

22. $4x^2 + 4$ _____

23. $4x^2 + 8x + 4$ _____

24. $9x^2 - 81$ _____

25. $3x^3 + 4x^2 - 3x - 4$ _____

SKILLS PRACTICE 87
Chapter 10 Review
More Operations with Polynomials

NAME _____

DATE _____

Factor completely.

1. $3x^2 + 6x - 9$ _____

2. $x^4 - x^3 - 2x^2$ _____

3. $5x^2 - 125$ _____

4. $8x^2 - 28x + 12$ _____

5. $x(2x + 3) - 5(2x + 3)$ _____

6. $x^2(x - 2) - 4(x - 2)$ _____

7. $8x(3x + 1) - (3x + 1)$ _____

8. $(x^2 + 3x)(2x - 1) + 2(2x - 1)$ _____

9. $2x^3 + 3x^2 + 2x + 3$ _____

10. $x^3 + 3x^2 - 9x - 27$ _____

11. $3x^3 + 3x^2 - 4x - 12$ _____

12. $x^3 + 3x^2 - 4x - 12$ _____

13. $6x^2 - x - 15$ _____

14. $15x^2 + 22x - 5$ _____

15. $9x^2 - 3x - 2$ _____

Solve by factoring then using the converse of the multiplication
property of zero. If prime, use the quadratic formula.

16. $x^2 + 7x + 12 = 0$ _____

17. $x^2 - 7x - 12 = 0$ _____

18. $x^2 - x = 20$ _____

19. $x^2 = 3x + 4$ _____

20. Find the GCF of the 2 polynomials $x^2 - 4$ and $2x^2 - 10x + 12$

_____

SKILLS PRACTICE 88
For use with Section 11-1
Introduction to Rational Algebraic
Expressions and Equations

NAME _____

DATE _____

Replace the variable with the given value. Write the result as a reduced fraction.

1. Evaluate $\dfrac{x+8}{x-6}$

   a. if x is 0 _____

   b. if x is 6 _____

   c. if x is 10 _____

2. Evaluate $\dfrac{x^2-5x+6}{x^2-9}$

   a. if x is 1 _____

   b. if x is -2 _____

   c. if x is 3 _____

Perform the indicated operations with the given fractions. Use the correct order of operations if more than one operation is involved. Write all fractions in lowest terms.

3. $\dfrac{3}{4}+\dfrac{3}{4}$ _____

4. $\dfrac{3}{4}+\dfrac{1}{3}$ _____

5. $\dfrac{3}{4}-\dfrac{1}{3}$ _____

6. $\left(\dfrac{3}{4}\right)\left(\dfrac{3}{4}\right)$ _____

7. $\left(\dfrac{2}{5}\right)^2-\dfrac{11}{15}$ _____

8. $\dfrac{5}{6}-\left(\dfrac{2}{3}\right)\left(\dfrac{9}{10}\right)$ _____

9. $\dfrac{3}{8}\div\dfrac{3}{5}$ _____

10. $\dfrac{3}{5}\left(\dfrac{4}{15}-\dfrac{7}{30}\right)$ _____

11. $\dfrac{4-8}{4-2}$ _____

12. $\dfrac{7}{83}\div\dfrac{7}{83}$ _____

13. $\dfrac{7}{8}-\dfrac{3}{4}$ _____

14. $\dfrac{7}{8}\div\dfrac{3}{4}$ _____

15. $\dfrac{6}{7}\div2$ _____

16. $\dfrac{12}{17}\cdot34$ _____

17. $2-\left(\dfrac{2}{3}\right)^2+\dfrac{5}{9}$ _____

18. $\dfrac{13}{15}\cdot\dfrac{5}{26}$ _____

19. $\dfrac{5}{6}-\dfrac{2}{3}+\dfrac{1}{4}$ _____

Solve by factoring.

20. $x^2-x-2=0$ _____

21. $x^2-3x-4=0$ _____

22. $x^2-5x+6=0$ _____

23. $x^2-11x+18=0$ _____

24. $x^2+4x+4=0$ _____

SKILLS PRACTICE 89
For use with Section 11-2
Review of Adding, Subtracting, and
Multiplying Fractions

NAME _____

DATE _____

1. a. What is the difference between a term and a factor? _____

  b. Why can common factors in both numerator and denominator
  of fractions be ''canceled'' out?

  _____

Reduce by factoring and cancelling common factors.

2. $\dfrac{12x^2y}{8xy^2}$ _____

3. $\dfrac{8xy}{4x}$ _____

4. $\dfrac{15x^2}{5x}$ _____

5. $\dfrac{3(x + 2)}{6}$ _____

6. $\dfrac{6(2x - 3)}{3x}$ _____

7. $\dfrac{8x^2(4x - y)}{4xy}$ _____

8. $\dfrac{x^2 - 3x}{x}$ _____

9. $\dfrac{2x - 4}{2}$ _____

10. $\dfrac{6x^2 - 12x}{4(x - 2)}$ _____

11. $\dfrac{4x - 8}{4x}$ _____

12. $\dfrac{(x + 2)(x - 3)}{x + 2}$ _____

13. $\dfrac{(2x + 1)(x - 6)}{2x(x - 6)}$ _____

14. $\dfrac{4x^2 - 8}{x^2 - 2}$ _____

15. $\dfrac{x^2 - 4}{x^2 - 4x + 4}$ _____

16. $\dfrac{x^2 - 3x + 2}{x^2 - 5x + 6}$ _____

17. $\dfrac{2x - 6}{4x + 24}$ _____

18. $\dfrac{x^2 - 6x + 9}{x^2 - 9}$ _____

19. $\dfrac{x^2 - x - 2}{x^2 + 2x + 1}$ _____

20. $\dfrac{6x^3 - 6x^2}{6x - 6}$ _____

For the rational expression $\dfrac{x - 2}{x + 4}$

21. For what value of x is the fraction equivalent to 0? _____

22. What value of x would make the fraction undefined? _____

23. Evaluate the fraction if x is 6. _____

24. Can the expression be reduced? If so, do so. If not, explain why
   not.

   _____

25. Write an example of a prime quadratic binomial. _____

Multiply or divide the following rational expressions. Write all answers
in lowest terms with no grouping symbols.

1. $\dfrac{12x}{10y} \cdot \dfrac{5y^2}{x}$ _____

2. $\dfrac{2(x + 2)}{12} \cdot \dfrac{6x}{x + 2}$ _____

3. $\dfrac{x + 4}{4} \cdot \dfrac{8}{x^2 - 16}$ _____

4. $\dfrac{4x - 8}{x^2 - 4} \cdot \dfrac{x + 2}{8}$ _____

5. $\dfrac{5x}{x - 5} \cdot \dfrac{x^2 - 10x + 25}{25x^2}$ _____

6. $\dfrac{x^2 - 5x + 6}{6} \div \dfrac{x^2 - 4}{4}$ _____

7. $\dfrac{9}{x^2 - 9} \cdot \dfrac{x^2 - 6x + 9}{x}$ _____

8. $\dfrac{4x + 2}{8x} \div \dfrac{8x + 4}{8x}$ _____

9. $\dfrac{x^2 - 10x + 25}{x^2 - 5x} \cdot \dfrac{12x^2}{x^2 - 5x}$ _____

10. $\dfrac{3x(x - 1)}{15x^2 + 15} \cdot \dfrac{x^2 + 1}{(x - 1)^2}$ _____

11. $\dfrac{x}{x + 3} \div \dfrac{3x}{3 + x}$ _____

12. $(x + 2) \cdot \dfrac{8}{8x^2 + 16x}$ _____

13. $\dfrac{6x - 6}{3x + 6} \div \dfrac{8x}{x^2 + x - 2}$ _____

14. $\dfrac{x^2 - 9}{8x^2 - 16x - 24} \cdot \dfrac{8}{3x + 9}$ _____

15. $\dfrac{x^2 + x - 2}{x^2 - 4x + 3} \cdot \dfrac{x + 3}{x + 2}$ _____

16. $\dfrac{(2x)^3}{6x^2} \div \dfrac{xy^2}{6y}$ _____

17. $\dfrac{2x + 4}{2} \cdot \dfrac{6}{3x + 6}$ _____

18. $\dfrac{x^2 + x - 6}{9x} \div \dfrac{x^2 - 4}{x}$ _____

19. $\dfrac{3x^3 + 5x^2}{9x + 9} \cdot \dfrac{4x + 4}{3xy + 5y}$ _____

20. $\dfrac{9x^2 - 81}{x^2 + 5x + 6} \cdot \dfrac{x + 2}{18x}$ _____

Add or subtract.

21. $\dfrac{5}{6} - \dfrac{2}{3}$ _____

22. $\dfrac{5}{6} + \dfrac{2}{3}$ _____

23. $\dfrac{7}{8} - \dfrac{5}{4}$ _____

24. $\dfrac{1}{4} - \dfrac{1}{3}$ _____

25. $\dfrac{4}{5} + \dfrac{5}{6}$ _____

SKILLS PRACTICE 91

For use with Section 11-4
Multiplying Rational Expressions

NAME _____

DATE _____

State the **a.** Greatest Common Factor (GCF) and **b.** Lowest Common
Multiple (LCM). Leave the LCM in factored form.

1. $3x$, $9x$ _____

2. 8, $12x$ _____

3. x^5, $5x^4$, $3x^2$ _____

4. $3x$, $6x$, 8 _____

5. $6v$, $6v - 30$ _____

6. $r + 5$, $r^2 + 5r$ _____

7. $x^2 - x - 30$, $x^2 - 36$ _____

8. $x^2 + 8x + 7$, $x + 7$ _____

9. $x - 5$, $x^2 - 7x + 10$ _____

10. 5, $5x^2 - 20$, $10x^2 + 10x - 20$ _____

a. State the Least Common Denominator (LCD).
b. Write each fraction as an equivalent fraction with the LCD.
c. Add the fractions and reduce if possible.

11. $\dfrac{1}{x} + \dfrac{2}{x^2} + \dfrac{3}{x^3}$ _____

12. $\dfrac{5}{3x} + \dfrac{4}{2x}$ _____

13. $\dfrac{x}{8} + \dfrac{5x}{12}$ _____

14. $\dfrac{7}{8xy} + \dfrac{3}{4x} - \dfrac{2}{2y}$ _____

15. $\dfrac{x}{8} + \dfrac{x + 2}{6}$ _____

16. $\dfrac{x}{8} - \dfrac{x - 6}{6}$ _____

17. $\dfrac{2x}{3y} + \dfrac{3 - xy}{6y^2}$ _____

18. $\dfrac{5}{6x} + \dfrac{4}{3x^2} - \dfrac{x}{12}$ _____

19. $\dfrac{5}{3x} - \dfrac{7}{6x} + \dfrac{x}{9}$ _____

20. $\dfrac{3}{10x^2} - \dfrac{x - 3}{5x}$ _____

Add or subtract.

21. $\dfrac{5}{6} - \dfrac{3}{4}$ _____

22. $\dfrac{8}{9} - \dfrac{5}{6}$ _____

23. $\dfrac{4}{5} + \dfrac{5}{4}$ _____

24. $\dfrac{3}{7} + \dfrac{7}{3}$ _____

25. $\dfrac{7}{19} - \dfrac{7}{19}$ _____

a. State the Least Common Denominator (LCD).
b. Write each fraction as an equivalent fraction with the LCD.
c. Add the fractions and reduce if possible.

1. $\dfrac{4}{x-2} + \dfrac{2}{x-2}$ _____

2. $\dfrac{4x}{x-3} - \dfrac{x+4}{x-3}$ _____

3. $\dfrac{2}{x-2} + \dfrac{3}{2x-4}$ _____

4. $\dfrac{2x}{x-2} - \dfrac{3x}{2x-4}$ _____

5. $\dfrac{5}{4} - \dfrac{3}{x} + \dfrac{2}{x^2}$ _____

6. $\dfrac{2}{x^2-4} - \dfrac{x+1}{x+2}$ _____

7. $\dfrac{5x}{8} + \dfrac{3}{x} - \dfrac{4}{6x}$ _____

8. $\dfrac{1}{x-2} + \dfrac{1}{x+3}$ _____

9. $\dfrac{x^2}{x-3} - \dfrac{9}{x-3}$ _____

10. $\dfrac{x}{x-3} - \dfrac{5}{x+2}$ _____

11. $\dfrac{2}{x+4} + \dfrac{4}{x+2}$ _____

12. $\dfrac{x+1}{x} - \dfrac{x}{x+1}$ _____

13. $\dfrac{3}{5x} - \dfrac{6}{x^2} + \dfrac{3}{4}$ _____

14. $\dfrac{7}{x-2} + \dfrac{x}{x+3}$ _____

15. $\dfrac{x^2}{2x+2} + \dfrac{x}{x+1} + \dfrac{1}{2x+2}$ _____

16. $\dfrac{5}{6x} - \dfrac{7}{3x} + \dfrac{2}{3x^2-6x}$ _____

17. $\dfrac{8}{x+3} - \dfrac{2}{x^2+4x+3}$ _____

18. $\dfrac{x}{3x-9} - \dfrac{3}{x^2-3x}$ _____

19. $\dfrac{x+3}{x-1} - \dfrac{x}{x^2-2x+1}$ _____

20. $\dfrac{x}{2x-4} - \dfrac{2}{x^2-2x}$ _____

Factor.

21. $4x^2 + 4$ _____

22. $6x^2 - x - 15$ _____

23. $9x^2 - 3x - 2$ _____

24. $2x^3 + 3x^2 + 2x + 3$ _____

25. $x^3 + 3x^2 - 9x - 27$ _____

SKILLS PRACTICE 93
For use with Section 11-6
Combined Operations with
Rational Expressions

NAME _____

DATE _____

Do the indicated operations. Follow the correct order of operations.

1. $\dfrac{5}{x} - \dfrac{x}{y}$ _____

2. $\dfrac{5}{x} \cdot \dfrac{x}{y}$ _____

3. $\dfrac{5}{x} \div \dfrac{x}{y}$ _____

4. $\dfrac{2}{x + 2} + \dfrac{x + 2}{2}$ _____

5. $\dfrac{2}{x + 2} \cdot \dfrac{x^2 - 4}{4}$ _____

6. $\dfrac{2}{x - 2} - \dfrac{2}{x + 2}$ _____

7. $\dfrac{4x}{x - 3} + \dfrac{x}{x^2 - 2x - 3}$ _____

8. $\dfrac{4x}{x - 3} \div \dfrac{x}{x^2 - 2x - 3}$ _____

9. $\dfrac{5}{x + 3} - \dfrac{x - 1}{x - 2}$ _____

10. $\dfrac{x - 1}{x + 3} - \dfrac{2}{x - 2}$ _____

11. $\dfrac{1}{3} - \dfrac{3}{x} + \dfrac{x + 5}{x + 3}$ _____

12. $\dfrac{x^2 - 4}{x^2 + 4x} \cdot \dfrac{6x}{x + 2} \div \dfrac{x - 2}{x + 4}$ _____

13. $\dfrac{2}{x - 5} + \dfrac{x - 5}{2} \cdot \dfrac{4}{x^2 - 25}$ _____

14. $\dfrac{x^2 - 5x + 4}{x^2 - 1} \div \dfrac{x^2 + 1}{x^2 + 2x + 1} + 3$ _____

15. $\dfrac{9x^2 - 81}{27} \cdot \dfrac{36}{x^2 - 6x + 9}$ _____

16. $\dfrac{x^2 + 3x + 2}{3x} \div \dfrac{x^2 + 5x + 4}{6x^2}$ _____

17. $\dfrac{7x + 14}{28} + \dfrac{3x + 6}{12}$ _____

18. $\dfrac{1}{x + 2} - \dfrac{1}{x - 2}$ _____

19. $\dfrac{2x}{x + 3} + \dfrac{x}{x + 1}$ _____

20. $\dfrac{2x}{x + 3} \div \dfrac{x}{x + 1}$ _____

Simplify. Write with no powers of variables in the denominator.

21. $3x^3(2x^2)$ _____

22. $\dfrac{8x^6}{4x^2}$ _____

23. $(2x)^3$ _____

24. $3x^2(3x - 5) + 5x^3 - x^2$ _____

25. $\dfrac{2^{-3}x^3}{y^{-3}}$ _____

SKILLS PRACTICE 94
For use with Section 11-6
Combined Operations with
Rational Expressions

NAME _____

DATE _____

Perform the indicated operation and write the result in reduced form. If a "−1" is obtained by reducing, distribute it throughout the numerator of the resulting fraction.

1. $\dfrac{(x + 5)(x + 3)}{(5 + x)(x - 3)}$ _____

2. $\dfrac{(x + 5)(3 - x)}{(x + 5)(x - 3)}$ _____

3. $\dfrac{(2x + 4)(x + 3)}{(x + 3)(4x + 2)}$ _____

4. $\dfrac{9 - x^2}{x^2 - 6x + 9}$ _____

5. $\dfrac{x^2 - 4x - 5}{(2 - x)(x + 1)}$ _____

6. $\dfrac{8}{x - 2} - \dfrac{4x}{x - 2}$ _____

7. $\dfrac{8}{x - 2} \div \dfrac{4x}{x - 2}$ _____

8. $\dfrac{-3x}{x - 3} \div \dfrac{9}{3 - x}$ _____

9. $\dfrac{-3x}{x - 3} + \dfrac{9}{3 - x}$ _____

10. $\dfrac{x^2 + 2x + 1}{x^2 - 1} \cdot \dfrac{9 - x^2}{x^2 - 2x - 3}$ _____

11. $\dfrac{2}{2x + 1} + \dfrac{2}{x + 1}$ _____

12. $\dfrac{2}{2x + 1} \div \dfrac{2}{x + 1}$ _____

13. $\dfrac{x + 1}{x - 3} + \dfrac{x - 3}{x + 1}$ _____

14. $\dfrac{3}{x} + \dfrac{2}{3x} + \dfrac{x}{6}$ _____

15. $\dfrac{3}{x} \div \dfrac{2}{3x} - \dfrac{x}{6}$ _____

16. $\dfrac{2}{x^2 - 4} - \dfrac{x}{x^2 - 4}$ _____

17. $\dfrac{4}{x + 1} + \dfrac{4x}{x + 1}$ _____

18. $\dfrac{5x}{6} - \dfrac{4x^2}{9} \cdot \dfrac{6}{8x}$ _____

19. $\dfrac{2 - x}{x^2 - 5x + 6} \cdot \dfrac{x^2 - 9}{9}$ _____

20. $\dfrac{x}{3} - \dfrac{7}{x} \div \dfrac{7}{6x}$ _____

For the expression $|x - 5|$,

21. Evaluate the expression if x is 9. _____

22. Evaluate the expression if x is −9. _____

23. Find the value of x if the expression is 9. _____

24. Find the value of x if the expression is −9. _____

25. Solve the equation $(x - 5)^2 = 9$. _____

Divide and express the remainder as a fraction added to the quotient.

1. $\dfrac{x^2 + 5x + 6}{x + 1}$ _____

2. $\dfrac{x^2 + 6x + 5}{x + 2}$ _____

3. $\dfrac{x^2 + 5x + 6}{x - 1}$ _____

4. $\dfrac{x^2 - 3x + 2}{x + 3}$ _____

5. $\dfrac{x^2 + 5x + 6}{x + 2}$ _____

6. $\dfrac{x^2 + 3x - 5}{x - 4}$ _____

7. $\dfrac{x^2 - 5x + 4}{x - 3}$ _____

8. $\dfrac{x^2 - 6x + 7}{x + 4}$ _____

9. $\dfrac{x^2 + 6x + 8}{x - 3}$ _____

10. $\dfrac{x^2 - 3x + 5}{x + 1}$ _____

11. $\dfrac{x^2 - 6x - 6}{x - 1}$ _____

12. $\dfrac{x^2 - 5x + 3}{x + 2}$ _____

13. $\dfrac{x^2 + 7x - 5}{x - 5}$ _____

14. $\dfrac{x^2 + 6x - 4}{x - 4}$ _____

15. $\dfrac{x^2 + 8x + 8}{x + 2}$ _____

16. $\dfrac{x^2 + 6x + 6}{x + 3}$ _____

17. $\dfrac{x^2 - 9x - 10}{x - 10}$ _____

18. $\dfrac{x^2 - 9x + 10}{x - 1}$ _____

19. $\dfrac{x^2 + 1}{x + 1}$ _____

20. $\dfrac{x^2 + 4}{x + 2}$ _____

Simplify.

21. $(3x - 2)^2$ _____

22. $(3x - 2)(3x + 2)$ _____

23. $3(5x - 4) - (6x - 8)$ _____

24. $3[2 - (3x + 5)]$ _____

25. $4x - (x + 8)^2$ _____

State the values of x for which the fraction cannot be defined.

1. $\dfrac{x}{x + 2}$ _____

2. $\dfrac{2x}{x - 3}$ _____

3. $\dfrac{x + 2}{x - 4}$ _____

4. $\dfrac{2x - 5}{x + 3}$ _____

5. $\dfrac{x - 1}{x^2 - 3x - 4}$ _____

6. $\dfrac{2x + 7}{x^2 + 7x + 12}$ _____

State the Least Common Multiple of all the denominators.
Leave polynomials in factored form.

7. $\dfrac{1}{x} + \dfrac{2}{5} = \dfrac{1}{10x}$ _____

8. $\dfrac{2}{x} + \dfrac{3}{2x} = 6$ _____

9. $\dfrac{2}{x + 2} + \dfrac{3}{2} = \dfrac{5}{x}$ _____

10. $\dfrac{5}{x + 5} + \dfrac{2}{x^2 - 25} = \dfrac{3}{x - 5}$ _____

11. $\dfrac{2}{x - 2} + \dfrac{2}{x^2 - 4x + 4} = \dfrac{3}{x + 2}$ _____

12. $\dfrac{x}{x^2 - 9} + \dfrac{3}{x + 3} = \dfrac{x}{x^2 - 5x + 6}$ _____

a. State the restrictions on the values of x.
b. State the LCM of all the denominators.
c. Multiply all members of the equation by the LCM.
d. Solve the resulting equation and check for extraneous solutions.

13. $\dfrac{8}{x - 3} = \dfrac{2}{3}$ _____

14. $\dfrac{4}{x + 5} = \dfrac{2}{5}$ _____

15. $\dfrac{x}{2x + 1} = \dfrac{3}{5}$ _____

16. $\dfrac{2}{x + 1} = \dfrac{x}{3}$ _____

17. $\dfrac{2}{x} + \dfrac{1}{2} = \dfrac{3}{2}$ _____

18. $\dfrac{3}{x} + \dfrac{1}{5} = \dfrac{6}{5}$ _____

19. $\dfrac{2}{x + 1} + \dfrac{3}{x - 1} = \dfrac{5}{x^2 - 1}$ _____

20. $\dfrac{2}{x - 2} + \dfrac{5x}{x + 2} = 5$ _____

For the equation $2x - 3y = 12$

21. State the x-intercept. _____

22. State the y-intercept. _____

23. State the slope of the line. _____

24. Graph the line. _____

SKILLS PRACTICE 97

For use with Section 11-9
Fractional Equations and Extraneous
Solutions

NAME _____

DATE _____

Find the value of the variable.

1. $2{:}x = 4{:}6$ _____

2. $6{:}x = 10{:}8$ _____

3. $x{:}6 = 6{:}12$ _____

4. $x{:}8 = 4{:}5$ _____

5. $5{:}4 = x{:}12$ _____

6. $7{:}8 = x{:}100$ _____

7. $x{:}4 = 9{:}x$ _____

8. $5{:}x = x{:}20$ _____

Write the ratios in lowest terms.

9. $6{:}8$ _____

10. $15{:}35$ _____

11. $30{:}45$ _____

12. $125{:}75$ _____

Write a proportion to describe the situation. Solve it to answer the
question.

13. The ratio of 2 integers is 2 to 5. If the smaller integer is 40, what
is the larger integer?

_____

14. The ratio of 2 integers is 6 to 13. If the smaller integer is 78, find
the larger integer.

_____

15. The ratio of 2 integers is 17 to 20. If the larger integer is 900,
find the smaller integer.

_____

16. The ratio of 2 integers is 5 to 8. If the sum of the 2 integers is
104, find the smaller integer.

_____

17. The ratio of 2 integers is 14 to 9. If the sum of the 2 integers is
345, find the larger integer.

_____

18. Sam sorted candy in a large bag of candy by color. He
found that 5 out of 24 pieces of candy were green. If this ratio
continues, how many green pieces of candy will there be in a
gigantic bag of 360 pieces?

State the axiom which justifies each of the following:

19. $x + a = a + x$ _____

20. $a(x + y) = ax + ay$ _____

21. If $x = y$ and $y = z$, then $x = z$. _____

22. $x = x$ _____

Write an expression to describe the quantity specified.

1. It takes Lesa 25 minutes to do her homework consisting of
p problems. What is the rate at which she does her work?

_____

2. Russell can ride his bicycle x miles in 3 minutes. What is the rate
at which he rides?

_____

3. James can do x situps in 5 minutes. How many situps does he do
per minute?

_____

4. At his new job, Carlos can wash 35 dishes in x minutes. What is
his rate of dish washing?

_____

Set up an equation describing the situation and solve it.

5. If 2 people work on the same task, their combined rate of work
will be the sum of the individual rates. Scott can mow a lawn in 3
hours and Roger can mow that same lawn in 2 hours. If they work
together, how long will it take them to mow that lawn?

_____

6. Edward can run from the school to the local convenience mart
in 4 minutes. Matt takes 5 minutes to run the same distance. If
Edward starts at the school and Matt starts at the convenience mart
at the same time and they run toward each other, how many
minutes will pass before they pass each other?

_____

7. Darren was out canoeing in the Guadalupe River where the current
flows at a rate of 4 ft per second. Darren paddles at a rate of 5 ft
per second on still water. How long will it take him to paddle a
round trip of 1200 feet?

_____

8. If you pick a card at random out of a standard bridge deck of 52
cards, what is the probability that you select a

a. diamond? _____

b. 10? _____

c. the 10 of diamonds? _____

9. A jar has 25 pieces of candy, 12 of which are red and 13 of which
are green. If Arden picks one at random, what is the probability
that she selects

a. a green piece of candy? _____   **c.** a purple piece of candy? _____

b. a red piece of candy? _____   **d.** a red or green piece of candy? _____

Perform the indicated operation. Write the result as a reduced fraction.

1. $\dfrac{3}{4} + \dfrac{4}{9}$ _____

2. $\dfrac{3}{4} \cdot \dfrac{4}{9}$ _____

3. $\dfrac{4}{3x} + \dfrac{2}{x}$ _____

4. $\dfrac{5}{x} + \dfrac{x}{x+2}$ _____

5. $\dfrac{2}{x} \cdot \dfrac{x}{x+2}$ _____

6. $\dfrac{2x}{x+2} + \dfrac{4}{x+2}$ _____

7. $\dfrac{3}{x^2-4} + \dfrac{4}{2x+4}$ _____

8. $\dfrac{x^2-6x-7}{x-1} \cdot \dfrac{x^2-1}{x^2+4x+3}$ _____

9. $\dfrac{4-x^2}{x^2+5x+6} \cdot \dfrac{x^2-10x+9}{x^2-3x+2}$ _____

10. $\dfrac{2x^2-x-1}{9x^3} \div \dfrac{x^2+x-2}{6x^2}$ _____

11. $\dfrac{3}{x+2} - \dfrac{x^2+4x+3}{x^2-4} \div \dfrac{1+x}{2-x}$ _____

12. Evaluate the fraction $\dfrac{2x-6}{x+2}$ if x is

a. 2 _____   **b.** 3 _____   **c.** -2 _____

a. State the restrictions on x.
b. State the LCD of all the denominators.
c. Solve the equation.
d. Check for extraneous solutions.

13. $\dfrac{5}{x+2} = \dfrac{3}{x}$ _____

14. $\dfrac{x+2}{4x} - \dfrac{5}{8} = \dfrac{3}{2x}$ _____

15. $\dfrac{4}{x+4} + \dfrac{x}{4+x} = 2$ _____

16. Find x in the proportion $3:5 = 4:x$. _____

17. Two numbers are in a ratio of 8 to 12. If the larger number is 42, the smaller number is

_____ ?

18. Two numbers are in a ratio of 12 to 17. If the sum of the numbers is 435, find the larger number.

_____

19. It takes Frank 3 hours to do a job. If Eddie works with him, it takes him only 2 hours. What is Eddie's rate?

_____

SKILLS PRACTICE 100
For use with Section 12-2
Sums, Differences, and Products of Radicals

NAME _____

DATE _____

1. Find the integers from 1 to 144 which are perfect squares and write the square root of each one. _____

Write in simple radical form.

2. $\sqrt{8}$ _____

3. $\sqrt{18}$ _____

4. $\sqrt{24}$ _____

5. $\sqrt{27}$ _____

6. $\sqrt{32}$ _____

7. $\sqrt{40}$ _____

8. $\sqrt{45}$ _____

9. $\sqrt{48}$ _____

10. $\sqrt{162}$ _____

11. $\sqrt{75}$ _____

12. $\sqrt{192}$ _____

13. $\sqrt{225}$ _____

Multiply and write in simple radical form.

14. $\sqrt{5} \cdot \sqrt{10}$ _____

15. $\sqrt{3} \cdot \sqrt{20}$ _____

16. $\sqrt{7} \cdot \sqrt{14}$ _____

17. $\sqrt{6} \cdot \sqrt{15}$ _____

18. $\sqrt{8} \cdot \sqrt{12}$ _____

19. $\sqrt{5} \cdot \sqrt{30}$ _____

20. $2\sqrt{5} \cdot \sqrt{10}$ _____

21. $3\sqrt{3} \cdot \sqrt{20}$ _____

22. $4\sqrt{6} \cdot \sqrt{15}$ _____

23. $9\sqrt{6} \cdot \sqrt{24}$ _____

24. $2\sqrt{5} \cdot 3\sqrt{15}$ _____

25. $6\sqrt{6} \cdot 8\sqrt{8}$ _____

Add and write in simple radical form.

26. $\sqrt{5} + 2\sqrt{5}$ _____

27. $3\sqrt{3} - 5\sqrt{3}$ _____

28. $4\sqrt{6} + 5\sqrt{6}$ _____

29. $7\sqrt{5} - \sqrt{5}$ _____

30. $\sqrt{8} + \sqrt{8}$ _____

31. $2\sqrt{8} + 3\sqrt{8}$ _____

32. $\sqrt{12} + \sqrt{27}$ _____

33. $\sqrt{18} - \sqrt{8}$ _____

34. $3\sqrt{24} - 4\sqrt{54}$ _____

35. $4\sqrt{12} - 5\sqrt{27} + \sqrt{24}$ _____

36. What is the least common multiple of x^2, $8xy^3$, $x^2 - x$? _____

37. What is the greatest common factor of $x^2 - 4$ and $x^2 - 4x + 4$? _____

Write in lowest terms.

38. $\dfrac{1}{3x} + \dfrac{2}{x^2}$ _____

39. $\dfrac{x^2 - 5x + 6}{3x^2 - 27}$ _____

Write in simple radical form with no radicals in the denominator.

1. $\dfrac{1}{\sqrt{2}}$ _____

2. $\dfrac{3}{\sqrt{4}}$ _____

3. $\dfrac{\sqrt{5}}{\sqrt{3}}$ _____

4. $\dfrac{\sqrt{2}}{\sqrt{5}}$ _____

5. $\dfrac{\sqrt{6}}{\sqrt{15}}$ _____

6. $\dfrac{\sqrt{8}}{\sqrt{5}}$ _____

7. $\dfrac{\sqrt{6}}{\sqrt{50}}$ _____

8. $\dfrac{\sqrt{5}}{\sqrt{50}}$ _____

9. $\dfrac{2\sqrt{5}}{\sqrt{8}}$ _____

10. $\dfrac{3\sqrt{5}}{\sqrt{9}}$ _____

11. $\dfrac{4\sqrt{8}}{\sqrt{10}}$ _____

12. $\dfrac{3\sqrt{12}}{\sqrt{24}}$ _____

13. $\dfrac{\sqrt{25}}{\sqrt{14}}$ _____

14. $\dfrac{\sqrt{18}}{\sqrt{24}}$ _____

15. $\dfrac{\sqrt{5}}{\sqrt{27}}$ _____

16. $\dfrac{\sqrt{16}}{\sqrt{81}}$ _____

17. $\dfrac{\sqrt{45}}{\sqrt{20}}$ _____

18. $\dfrac{\sqrt{20}}{\sqrt{18}}$ _____

19. $\dfrac{5\sqrt{8}}{\sqrt{24}}$ _____

20. $\dfrac{4\sqrt{5}}{\sqrt{72}}$ _____

21. Add $\dfrac{1}{2} + \dfrac{2}{3} + \dfrac{4}{x}$. _____

22. Multiply $\dfrac{3}{4} \cdot \dfrac{5}{4}$. _____

23. Divide $\dfrac{x^2 + x - 2}{2x^5} \div \dfrac{x^2 - 1}{x^2 + 1}$. _____

24. Factor completely $9x^2 - 81$. _____

25. Factor completely $x^3 + x^2 - 4x - 4$. _____

Multiply and write in simple radical form.

1. $\sqrt{3}\,(1 + \sqrt{2})$ _____

2. $\sqrt{2}\,(\sqrt{3} + \sqrt{2})$ _____

3. $\sqrt{5}\,(\sqrt{10} + \sqrt{15})$ _____

4. $\sqrt{6}\,(\sqrt{3} + \sqrt{2})$ _____

5. $(1 + \sqrt{2})(1 + \sqrt{2})$ _____

6. $(2 - \sqrt{3})(3 + \sqrt{3})$ _____

7. $(2 - \sqrt{3})(2 + \sqrt{3})$ _____

8. $(6 - \sqrt{7})(6 + \sqrt{7})$ _____

9. $(\sqrt{3} + \sqrt{2})(\sqrt{3} + \sqrt{2})$ _____

10. $(\sqrt{3} - \sqrt{2})(\sqrt{3} + \sqrt{2})$ _____

11. $(4 + \sqrt{5})(4 + \sqrt{5})$ _____

12. $(4 + \sqrt{5})^2$ _____

13. $(2 - \sqrt{3})^2$ _____

14. $(2 + \sqrt{3})^2$ _____

15. $(\sqrt{2} + \sqrt{3})^2$ _____

16. $(\sqrt{2} - \sqrt{3})^2$ _____

Rationalize the denominators.

17. $\dfrac{1}{\sqrt{2}}$ _____

18. $\dfrac{\sqrt{3}}{\sqrt{2}}$ _____

19. $\dfrac{\sqrt{3}}{\sqrt{3} - 2}$ _____

20. $\dfrac{\sqrt{2} + \sqrt{3}}{\sqrt{2} - \sqrt{3}}$ _____

Simplify.

21. $\sqrt{320}$ _____

22. $\sqrt{45} + \sqrt{20}$ _____

23. $4\sqrt{8} - \sqrt{8}$ _____

24. $4\sqrt{6} \cdot 5\sqrt{12}$ _____

25. $5\sqrt{12} + 4\sqrt{32} - 5\sqrt{27}$ _____

For use with Section 12-6
Radical Equations

Solve.

1. $\sqrt{x + 5} = 6$ _____

2. $\sqrt{x - 5} = 6$ _____

3. $\sqrt{3x} = 6$ _____

4. $\sqrt{2x + 1} = 5$ _____

5. $\sqrt{x} + 5 = 6$ _____

6. $\sqrt{x} - 5 = 6$ _____

7. $\sqrt{2x} + 1 = 5$ _____

8. $7 + \sqrt{x} = 8$ _____

9. $8 + \sqrt{x} = 7$ _____

10. $\sqrt{3x + 1} = 5$ _____

11. $\sqrt{x + 3} = 3$ _____

12. $\sqrt{x - 3} = 3$ _____

13. $\sqrt{5x - 3} = 6$ _____

14. $8 + \sqrt{x + 8} = 9$ _____

15. $\sqrt{3x - 4} + 10 = 6$ _____

16. $7 - \sqrt{x} = 6$ _____

17. $\sqrt{5x + 4} = 7$ _____

18. $\sqrt{x} - 8 = 0$ _____

19. $4 + \sqrt{2x} = 6$ _____

20. $\sqrt{5 - x} = 4$ _____

Simplify. Rationalize all denominators.

21. $\sqrt{28}$ _____

22. $\sqrt{8} - 3\sqrt{8}$ _____

23. $\sqrt{5} \cdot 3\sqrt{10}$ _____

24. $\dfrac{\sqrt{15}}{\sqrt{8}}$ _____

25. $\dfrac{\sqrt{2}}{1 - \sqrt{2}}$ _____

Using the Pythagorean Theorem, find the length of the third side of each of the following triangles. Round approximate answers to 2 decimal places.

1. 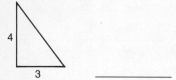 _____

2. 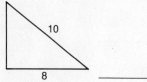 _____

3. 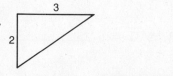 _____

4. 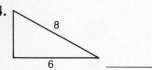 _____

5. 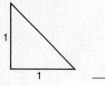 _____

6. 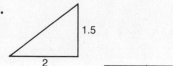 _____

7. 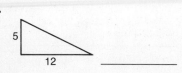 _____

8. 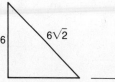 _____

9. 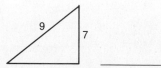 _____

10. 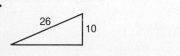 _____

11. _____

12. _____

13. 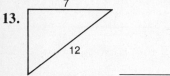 _____

14. 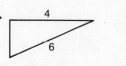 _____

15. 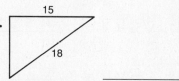 _____

16. 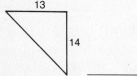 _____

17. 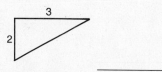 _____

18. 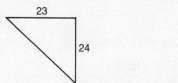 _____

19. _____

20. 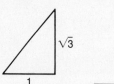 _____

Simplify.

21. $(\sqrt{2} + 3)^2$ _____

22. $(\sqrt{2} + 3)(\sqrt{2} - 3)$ _____

23. $\sqrt{8} - \sqrt{18}$ _____

24. $5\sqrt{12} \cdot 3\sqrt{24}$ _____

25. $\sqrt{16 + 9}$ _____

Write the radical as an expression with a fractional exponent.

1. $\sqrt[3]{5}$ _____

2. $\sqrt[4]{16}$ _____

3. $\sqrt[5]{12.3}$ _____

4. $\sqrt[2]{8}$ _____

5. $\sqrt[6]{128}$ _____

Use a calculator to evaluate. Round to 2 decimal places.

6. $\sqrt[3]{5}$ _____

7. $\sqrt[4]{16}$ _____

8. $\sqrt[5]{12.3}$ _____

9. $\sqrt[2]{8}$ _____

10. $\sqrt[6]{128}$ _____

11. $\sqrt[3]{125}$ _____

12. $\sqrt[3]{27}$ _____

13. $\sqrt[4]{81}$ _____

14. $\sqrt[2]{81}$ _____

15. $\sqrt[3]{81}$ _____

16. $\sqrt[2]{64}$ _____

17. $\sqrt[3]{64}$ _____

18. $\sqrt[4]{64}$ _____

19. $\sqrt[5]{64}$ _____

20. $\sqrt[6]{64}$ _____

Simplify.

21. $\sqrt{50}$ _____

22. $\dfrac{5}{\sqrt{50}}$ _____

23. $\dfrac{\sqrt{2}}{\sqrt{2} - 1}$ _____

24. $(4 + \sqrt{5})(4 - \sqrt{5})$ _____

25. Solve for x. $\sqrt{x} + 7 = 9$ _____

Write as either a terminating or a repeating decimal.

1. $\frac{3}{8}$ _____

2. $\frac{8}{3}$ _____

3. $\frac{5}{12}$ _____

4. $\frac{7}{9}$ _____

5. $\frac{9}{7}$ _____

6. $\frac{5}{16}$ _____

7. $\frac{1}{6}$ _____

8. $\frac{12}{5}$ _____

Write as a reduced fraction.

9. 0.333333333... _____

10. 0.66666666666... _____

11. 0.222222222... _____

12. 0.1616161616... _____

13. 0.888888888... _____

14. 0.0101010101... _____

Tell whether the given number is rational or irrational using the definition of a rational number.

15. $\sqrt[4]{64}$ _____

16. $\sqrt[6]{64}$ _____

17. 3.14 _____

18. π _____

19. 0.3 _____

20. 0.3333333... _____

For the radical expression $\sqrt{x - 5}$:

21. Evaluate if x is 13. (Write the result in simple radical form.)

_____

22. Find x if the expression is equal to 13. _____

23. If x is 9 is the result rational or irrational? Justify your answer.

24. Evaluate if x is 0. _____

25. Find x if the expression is equal to 0. _____

1. For the radical expression $\sqrt{x + 4}$:
   a. Evaluate the expression if x is 8. Write the result in simple radical form. Is the result rational or irrational?

   _____

   b. Evaluate the expression if x is 12. Write the result in simple radical form. Is the result rational or irrational?

   _____

   c. Find the value of x if the expression is equal to 7. _____

   d. Find the value of x if the expression is equal to -1. _____

Write in simple radical form.

2. $\sqrt{24}$ _____

3. $\sqrt{128}$ _____

4. $\sqrt{5} - 6\sqrt{5}$ _____

5. $\sqrt{12} + 3\sqrt{12}$ _____

6. $2\sqrt{24} - \sqrt{24}$ _____

7. $3\sqrt{8} \cdot 4\sqrt{12}$ _____

8. $\sqrt{27} + \sqrt{12}$ _____

9. $\sqrt{6} + \sqrt{3}$ _____

10. $(1 + \sqrt{2})^2$ _____

11. $(1 + \sqrt{2})(1 - \sqrt{2})$ _____

12. $\dfrac{6}{\sqrt{3}}$ _____

13. $\sqrt{\dfrac{3}{8}}$ _____

14. $(2 + \sqrt{3})(1 - \sqrt{6})$ _____

15. $\sqrt{16 + 9}$ _____

16. $\sqrt{24} \cdot \sqrt{18}$ _____

17. $\dfrac{2}{1 - \sqrt{3}}$ _____

18. Write each of the following repeating decimals as fractions.

   a. 0.5555555... _____

   b. 0.05050505... _____

19. Find the length of the third side in the following triangles.

   a.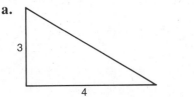

   _____

   b.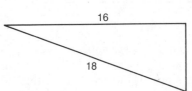

   _____

20. Evaluate the radical $\sqrt[x]{81}$ if x is

   a. 2 _____

   b. 3 _____

   c. 4 _____

   d. 5 _____

   e. Which of the results in a through d are rational? _____

Draw a number line graph of the inequality.

1. $x > 5$ _____

2. $x < -3$ _____

3. $x \geq -4$ _____

4. $x \leq 0$ _____

5. $x \geq -2\frac{1}{2}$ _____

6. $x > 7.5$ _____

7. $9 \leq x$ _____

8. $0 \geq x$ _____

9. $x < 7$ _____

Write an inequality for the given number line graph.

10. _____

11. _____

12. _____

13. _____

14. _____

15. _____

16. _____

17. _____

18. _____

19. _____

20. Graph the line $2x - 3y = 6$. _____

21. What is the slope of the line connecting the points $(2, 3)$ and $(-2, 4)$?

_____

22. What is the slope of the line $3x - 5y = 8$? _____

23. Name 3 points which are on the graph of the line $3x + 4y = 12$.

_____

a. Solve the inequality.
b. Sketch the solution on a number line.

1. $x + 2 > 5$ _____

2. $x + 5 > 2$ _____

3. $x - 8 \leq 9$ _____

4. $x - 7 \geq -6$ _____

5. $2x + 1 \geq 7$ _____

6. $3x - 5 < 16$ _____

7. $3x - 2 \leq -14$ _____

8. $-5 + 2x < -8$ _____

9. $5 - 2x \leq 7$ _____

10. $-3x + 7 \geq -8$ _____

11. $3x - 5 > x + 7$ _____

12. $4 - 4x \leq -6x + 10$ _____

13. $-1 + x \geq 27 - 6x$ _____

14. $4 < 8 - x$ _____

15. $2(x - 3) \geq x + 7$ _____

16. $5 - (x - 3) \leq 8$ _____

17. $5 - 2(4 - x) > 2x + 3$ _____

18. $8 + 6x < 4$ _____

19. $\left(\frac{1}{2}\right)x + 3 \geq -8$ _____

20. $5 \leq 8 + 5x$ _____

Solve.

21. $4x - 5 = 11$ _____

22. $(x + 3)^2 = 16$ _____

23. $x^2 + 2x - 3 = 0$ _____

24. $2(x + 3) = x - 8$ _____

25. $5x + 8 = -6x + 19$ _____

Sketch a number line graph of the compound inequality.

1. $-3 \leq x \leq 5$ _____

2. $x \geq -3$ and $x \leq 5$ _____

3. $x < -3$ or $x > 5$ _____

4. $x \leq 2$ or $x > 8$ _____

5. $2 \leq x < 8$ _____

6. $x < -5$ or $x \geq -3$ _____

7. x is between 1 and 7, inclusive. _____

8. x is less than -4 or x is greater than or equal to 6.

_____

9. x is not between nor equal to -2 and 4. _____

10. x is greater than 2 and x is less than 5. _____

Write a compound inequality to describe the inequality graphed.

11. _____

12. _____

13. _____

14. _____

15. _____

Solve the compound inequality and sketch the graph on a number line.

16. $x + 2 < 4$ or $x - 3 > 9$ _____

17. $x + 2 \geq 4$ and $x - 3 \leq 9$ _____

18. $4 < x - 5 < 9$ _____

19. $3 - 2x > 3$ or $2x - 3 > 9$ _____

20. $4 \leq 2x \leq 8$ _____

21. $-4 < 3x + 5 < 11$ _____

22. $5 < 1 - x \leq 8$ _____

23. $5 + x \geq -10$ and $x - 4 \leq 0$ _____

Consider the expression $|x - 9|$.

24. What kind of expression is it? _____

25. Evaluate the expression if x is 12. _____

26. Evaluate the expression if x is -12. _____

27. Find the value of x if the expression is equal to 4. _____

28. Find the value of x if the expression is equal to -4. _____

29. Find the value of x if the expression is equal to 0. _____

Using the words "between" and "not between," describe the absolute value inequalities. For example, $|x + 2| \geq 4$ in words would be "$x + 2$ is not between -4 and 4, inclusive."

1. $|x| < 3$ _____

2. $|x| > 6$ _____

3. $|2x + 1| \leq 8$ _____

4. $|2 - 3x| \geq 8$ _____

5. $|x + 5| > 3$ _____

6. $|x - 6| < 5$ _____

Write the absolute value inequality described by the symbols. For example, $-4 < x + 3 < 4$ would be $|x + 3| < 4$.

7. $x \leq -5$ or $x \geq 5$ _____

8. $x + 2 \geq -6$ and $x + 2 \leq 6$ _____

9. $x - 5$ is not between -7 and 7, inclusive. _____

10. $-9 \leq 2x - 3 \leq 8$ _____

Solve the absolute value inequalities and graph the result on the number line.

11. $|x| \leq 6$ _____

12. $|x| \geq 4$ _____

13. $|x + 3| > 6$ _____

14. $|x - 5| < 3$ _____

15. $|2x| \geq 4$ _____

16. $|3x| > 12$ _____

17. $|2x + 1| < 7$ _____

18. $|2x + 1| \geq 7$ _____

19. $|4 + x| < -6$ _____

20. $|12 - 17x| \geq -90$ _____

21. Look back at your work on Problems 19 and 20. In Problem 19, replace x with a number from your solution and see if it makes a true statement. In Problem 20, replace x with a number which is *not* in your solution and see if you get a *false* statement. If the results do not match your inequalities, take another look at why not.

_____

Consider the absolute value expression $|x + 5|$.

22. Find the value of the expression if x is 15. _____

23. Find the value of x if the expression is 15. _____

24. Find the value of the expression if x is -10. _____

25. Find the value of x if the expression is -10. _____

26. For what values of x will the expression be positive? _____

SKILLS PRACTICE 112
For use with Section 13-5
Inequalities: Given x,
Evaluate the Expression

NAME _____

DATE _____

Write an inequality which will have the given values of x as the solution.

1. If $x > 6$, find $2x$. _____

2. If $x < 4$, find $3x$. _____

3. If $x \geq -3$, find $x - 5$. _____

4. If $x \leq 0$, find $x + 5$. _____

5. If $x \leq 5$, find $-3x$. _____

6. If $x > -2$, find $-4x$. _____

7. If $x > 7$, find $2x + 3$. _____

8. If $x \leq -6$, find $3x - 5$. _____

9. If $x > 0$, find $4x - 3$. _____

10. If $x \leq 13$, find $-2x + 5$. _____

11. If $x \geq 2$, find $4 - x$. _____

12. If $x \geq -1$, find $2 - 3x$. _____

13. If $-2 < x < 4$, find $x + 5$. _____

14. If x is at most 6, find $4x + 3$. _____

15. If x is at least 0, find $100 - 6x$. _____

16. If x is no more than 100, find $45 + 3x$. _____

17. If $0 \leq x \leq 5$, find $2x + 4$. _____

18. If $-3 \leq x \leq 6$, find $3 - 2x$. _____

19. Suppose you have taken a test on which you know that you got at least 15 questions correct but no more than 18 correct. If the grade is obtained by multiplying 5 times the number correct, give your range of possible grades.

_____

20. Suppose that your parents give you $30 a month to spend on buying lunches. On the average you spend about $2.50 each school day for lunch.
   a. If you buy lunches for d days, write an expression for the amount of lunch money remaining.

   _____

   b. If you want to have at least $8 lunch money remaining at the end of the month, what is the most number of times that you can buy your lunch? Please answer as a whole number.

_____

Solve.

21. $x + 3 \geq -5$ _____

22. $-5x + 7 < 22$ _____

23. $-4 < x + 3 < 9$ _____

24. $|x + 6| \leq 8$ _____

25. $|2x - 1| > 3$ _____

26. $|x + 9| \leq -5$ _____

Plot the graph of the inequality.

1. $y > 2x + 5$

2. $y < 4x - 6$

3. $y \geq 2x - 3$

4. $y \geq 3x + 1$

5. $y < -3x + 2$

6. $y > -4x + 2$

7. $2x + 3y \leq 6$

8. $2x + 3y > -6$

9. $x + 2y < 4$

10. $3x - y \geq 4$

11. $x - y \geq -5$

12. $2x - 3y \leq 12$

13. $-2x + y > 8$

14. $-3x - 4y \geq -4$

Plot the graph of the system of inequalities.

15. $y > x + 3$
$\quad y < -x + 7$

16. $y \leq -2x + 3$
$\quad y \leq -5x + 6$

17. $y > \left(\dfrac{2}{3}\right)x + 1$

$\quad y > -3x + 4$

18. $2x + y \leq -5$
$\quad x + 2y \geq -4$

19. $x - y > 0$
$\quad x + y < 0$

20. $x + 2y \geq -4$
$\quad x + 2y < 5$

21. Factor 288 into primes. _____

22. Evaluate $x^2 + 3x^3$ if x is -2. _____

23. Multiply $(2x - 1)^2$. _____

24. Multiply $(3x - 7)(3x + 7)$. _____

25. Simplify by distributing and adding common terms:
$\quad 3x(2x - 5) - (5x - 8)$.

_____

Write an inequality which will describe the number line graph.

1. _____

2. _____

3. _____

4. _____

5. _____

6. _____

7. _____

8. _____

9. _____

10. _____

Solve the inequality and sketch a graph of the solution on a number line.

11. $2x + 3 \geq 5$ **12.** $5 - 3x < 8$

13. $x - 5 \leq -9$ **14.** $-5 < x + 3 < 9$

15. $-2 < x < 4$ **16.** $x \geq 5$ or $x \leq -4$

17. $0 \leq 2x + 1 \leq 9$ **18.** $-3 < 2 - x < 4$

19. $2x + 5 \geq 13$ or $3x - 1 < -4$ **20.** $x + 8 > 9$ or $2x - 3 < -9$

21. $|x| \geq 4$ **22.** $|x| < 5$

23. $|2x + 1| \leq 7$ **24.** $|3 + 4x| > 7$

25. $|8x - 5| \leq -5$

Draw a graph of the inequality on a Cartesian coordinate plane.

26. $2x - 3y \leq -12$

27. $y > 2x - 5$
    $x + y < 7$

State whether or not the graphs drawn are functions.

1.

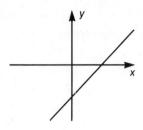

_____

2.

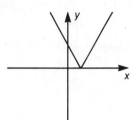

_____

3.

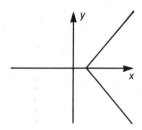

_____

4.

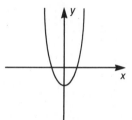

_____

a. Calculate the values of y for integer values of x in the interval given.

b. Plot the points on a graph and connect the points to continue the pattern.

5. $y = x + 3$ for $-4 \leq x \leq 4$

6. $y = -2x + 5$ for $-4 \leq x \leq 4$

7. $y = x^2$ for $-4 \leq x \leq 4$

8. $y = (x + 1)^2$ for $-4 \leq x \leq 4$

9. $y = x^2 + 1$ for $-4 \leq x \leq 4$

10. $y = |x|$ for $-4 \leq x \leq 4$

Graph on a number line.

11. $x \geq 3$

12. $2x + 5 < 8$

13. $-2 < x < 4$

14. $x < -8$ or $x > 7$

15. $|x + 2| \leq 4$

a. State whether the relationship is a direct or an inverse variation.
b. Using the given ordered pair, find the proportionality constant.

1. $y = kx$ (3, 6) _____

2. $y = \dfrac{k}{x}$ (3, 6) _____

3. $y = kx$ (−5, 8) _____

4. $y = \dfrac{k}{x}$ (−5, 8) _____

Write a variation function for each situation.

5. The number of dollars you earn depends on the number of hours you work.
_____

6. The length of time it takes to drive a certain distance depends on how fast you drive.
_____

7. The number of homework problems you do depends on how long you work.
_____

8. The number of homework problems you have done depends on how quickly you do each problem.
_____

9. The number of pages you read in a book depends on the number of hours you read.
_____

10. The distance between 2 cities depends on the length of the road as marked on a map.
_____

11. The distance traveled on a bicycle trip depends on the number of days you ride.
_____

12. You want to create a rectangle with an area of 24 square units. The length of the desired rectangle depends on the width you select.
_____

Solve.

13. $x + 2 = 9$ _____

14. $|x + 2| = 9$ _____

15. $(x + 2)^2 = 9$ _____

16. $\sqrt{x + 2} = 9$ _____

Use a calculator to find approximate values for the variable.

1. $\cos 30° = x$ _____

2. $\sin 75° = x$ _____

3. $\tan 48° = x$ _____

4. $\cos A = 0.5$ _____

5. $\sin A = 0.6156615$ _____

6. $\tan A = 1$ _____

Use the given trigonometric function to find the missing side.

7. cosine 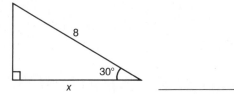 _____

8. cosine 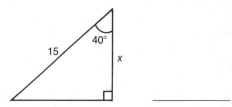 _____

9. sine 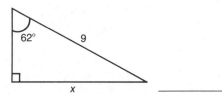 _____

10. sine 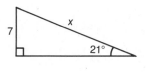 _____

11. tangent 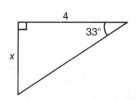 _____

12. tangent _____

13. You decide which function to use to find the missing side.

 _____

Use the given trigonometric function to find the indicated angle.

14. sine 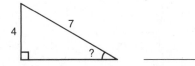 _____

15. sine 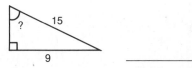 _____

16. cosine  _____

17. cosine 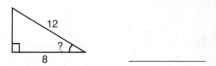 _____

18. tangent _____

19. tangent _____

Find the x-intercepts.

1. $y = x^2 - 3x - 4$ _____   **2.** $y = x^2 + 5x + 6$ _____

3. $y = x^2 - x - 2$ _____   **4.** $y = x^2 + 7x + 12$ _____

5. $y = x^2 - 4x + 4$ _____   **6.** $y = 2x^2 + x - 1$ _____

7. $y = x^2 - 6x + 5$ _____   **8.** $y = x^2 + x + 2$ _____

Find the y-intercepts.

9. $y = x^2 - x - 2$ _____   **10.** $y = x^2 + 7x + 12$ _____

11. $y = x^2 - 6x + 5$ _____   **12.** $y = x^2 + x + 2$ _____

Find the vertex.

13. $y = x^2 - 6x + 5$ _____   **14.** $y = x^2 + 8x - 4$ _____

15. $y = x^2 - 2x + 5$ _____   **16.** $y = x^2 + 4x - 3$ _____

17. $y = x^2 - 8x + 9$ _____   **18.** $y = x^2 + 4x - 2$ _____

19. $y = x^2 - 2x + 8$ _____   **20.** $y = x^2 + 10x$ _____

Perform the indicated operations.

21. $\dfrac{2}{x + 1} + \dfrac{3}{x^2 - 1}$ _____

22. $\dfrac{x^2 - 5x - 6}{x^2 - 9x + 18} \cdot \dfrac{9x - 27}{9x}$ _____

23. $\dfrac{x^2 - x - 6}{x^2 - 9} \div \dfrac{x^2 + 4x + 4}{x - 1}$ _____

24. $\dfrac{1}{x} + \dfrac{2}{x^2} - \dfrac{3}{x^3}$ _____

25. $\dfrac{x^2 + x - 6}{x^2 - 4}$ _____

SKILLS PRACTICE 119
For use with Section 14-6
Solving Quadratic Inequalities by Completing
the Square

NAME _____

DATE _____

Solve. Sketch the result on a number line.

1. $|x + 3| \le 4$

2. $|x - 4| > 5$

3. $|2x + 1| \ge 3$

4. $|2x - 1| < 5$

5. $|x + 7| \le 9$

6. $|3x + 4| > 7$

7. $|x - 9| \le -8$

8. $|x - 9| \ge 0$

Solve the quadratic inequality by taking the square root of both sides
of the inequality and then solving the resulting absolute value
inequality. Sketch the graph on a number line.

9. $(x + 2)^2 \ge 25$

10. $(x - 3)^2 < 16$

11. $(x - 4)^2 \le 9$

12. $(x - 1)^2 > 49$

13. $(x + 5)^2 \ge 9$

14. $(x - 6)^2 < 81$

15. $(x + 3)^2 \ge 16$

16. $(x + 7)^2 < 36$

Transform the inequality by completing the square. Sketch the final
result.

17. $x^2 - 2x - 8 \ge 0$

18. $x^2 + 2x - 8 < 0$

19. $x^2 - 6x + 8 \le 0$

20. $x^2 + 6x + 8 > 0$

21. Solve using the quadratic formula. $x^2 + 5x - 7 = 0$ _____

22. Solve by factoring. $x^2 - 5x + 6 = 0$ _____

23. Simplify $(2x - 3)^2$. _____

24. Write in simple radical form. $\sqrt{48}$ _____

25. Find the size of the marked angle in the given right triangle.

_____

SKILLS PRACTICE 120
For use with Section 14-7
Solving Quadratic Inequalities by the
Quadratic Formula

NAME _____

DATE _____

Sketch the graph using the end points for the given inequalities.

1. $x^2 + 7x + 12 \geq 0$

2. $x^2 - x - 6 < 0$

3. $x^2 + x - 6 \geq 0$

4. $x^2 + 4x - 45 < 0$

5. $x^2 - 3x - 4 \geq 0$

6. $x^2 - 10x + 16 > 0$

7. $x^2 - 11x + 18 \leq 0$

8. $x^2 - 3x - 10 \leq 0$

9. $x^2 + 7x + 13 > 0$

all real numbers

10. $-x^2 + 5x - 19 \geq 0$

$\varnothing$

Find the end points, if any, and sketch the graph.

11. $5x^2 - x - 1 > 0$

12. $5x^2 - x - 1 \leq 0$

13. $4x^2 + 5x - 8 \leq 0$

14. $-x^2 + 2x + 5 \geq 0$

15. $x^2 + x + 2 \leq 0$

16. For the quadratic function $y = x^2 - 4x - 5$,

    a. find the y-intercept _____

    b. find the x-intercept _____

    c. find the vertex _____

    d. sketch the function

17. Find the missing side of the right triangle.

18. Find the greatest common factor of $x^2 - 9$ and $x^2 - 5x + 6$.

_____

19. Find the least common multiple of $9x^2y$ and $18xy^3z$. _____

20. Find the value of the discriminant of the quadratic equation
$x^2 + 9x - 7 = 0$.

_____

1. For the quadratic function $y = x^2 + 2x - 3$
   a. sketch the function by finding

      i. the x-intercepts. _____

      ii. the y-intercept. _____

      iii. the vertex. _____
   b. If $y \geq 0$, sketch the result on a number line.
   c. If $y < 0$, sketch the result on a number line.

2. Sketch each of the following functions using integer values of x between -4 and 4, inclusive, to find the points which should be connected.

   a. $y = 2x - 3$ _____

   b. $y = |2x - 3|$ _____

   c. $y = (2x - 3)^2$ _____

Find the missing values of the given right triangles.

3.

_____

4.

_____

5.

_____

6.

_____

7.

_____

8.

_____

9. The number of miles that you can drive in your car depends on the number of gallons of fuel left in the tank. If you have 14 gallons in the tank, you can travel for 350 miles.
   a. Write a proportion which shows this relationship and find the proportionality constant.

      _____

   b. If the tank holds 14.6 gallons, how many miles can you drive?

      _____

   c. You have 58 more miles to go to complete a trip. You have 1.3 usable gallons of fuel left in the tank. Can you complete the trip without having to get more fuel?

      _____

1. State the axiom which justifies each of the following.
   a. $(3)(4) = (4)(3)$
   b. $(3 + 4) + 5 = 3 + (4 + 5)$
   c. If $3 = x$, then $x = 3$.
   d. $2(3 + x) = 6x + 2$

2. For the expression $3 - 2(3x - 4)$
   a. Simplify the expression.
   b. Evaluate the expression if x is -7.
   c. Find x if the expression is equal to -7.
   d. Find x if the expression is equal to $2x - 5$.

3. For the expression $(2x - 1)^2$
   a. Simplify the expression.
   b. Name the simplified expression by degree and number of terms.
   c. Evaluate the expression if x is -3.
   d. Find the value of x if the expression is equal to 25.

4. For the expression $|x - 6|$
   a. What kind of expression is this?
   b. Evaluate the expression if x is 8, -8
   c. Find the value of x if the expression is equal to 8, -8
   d. Find the value of x if the expression is less than or equal to 4.
   e. Find the value of x if the expression is greater than 5.

5. For the expression $2x^2 - 5x + 2$
   a. Evaluate the expression if x is -3.
   b. Factor the expression.
   c. Find the value of x if the expression is equal to 0.
   d. Find the value of x if the expression is equal to 1.
   e. If y equals the expression, sketch the graph of the equation.
   f. If the expression is greater than or equal to 0, sketch the solution on a number line.

6. For the line $2x - y = 8$
   a. i. What is the x-intercept of the line?
   ii. What is the y-intercept of the line?
   b. What is the slope of the line?
   c. Graph the line on a Cartesian coordinate plane.
   d. Where does the graph of the line $x + y = 7$ intersect the graph of the given line?
   e. Solve the system of equations created by using the equation $3x - 2y = 13$ and the given line.
   f. Graph the system of inequalities $2x - y \geq 8$
   $$x + y < 7$$

7. For the expression $\dfrac{x + 3}{x - 3}$,
   a. Evaluate the expression if x is
   i. 12
   ii. 3
   b. Find x if the expression equals -2.
   c. Find x if the expression equals $\frac{2}{3}$.

8. For the expression $\sqrt{2x - 4}$
   a. If $x = 8$, evaluate the expression and write the result in simple radical form.
   b. Evaluate the radical if x is 6.
   c. Are both of the answers in a and b rational? Why or why not?
   d. Find x if the expression is equal to 8.
   e. If $x = 5$, write the reciprocal of the expression in simple radical form with a rational denominator.

ANSWERS

SKILLS PRACTICE 1

1. $\frac{3}{4}$
2. $\frac{3}{7}$
3. $\frac{4}{15}$

4. $\frac{3}{2}$
5. 24
6. 48

7. 70
8. 20
9. $\frac{35}{4}$

10. $\frac{77}{6}$
11. $1\frac{8}{15}$
12. $1\frac{1}{2}$

13. 2
14. $\frac{2}{3}$
15. $\frac{1}{12}$

16. $16\frac{1}{4}$
17. $\frac{5}{8}$
18. $1\frac{1}{20}$

19. $15\frac{3}{4}$
20. $45\frac{1}{3}$
21. $\frac{4}{3}$

22. $\frac{2}{5}$
23. $\frac{7}{8}$
24. $\frac{8}{9}$

25. $3\frac{1}{3}$
26. 0.75
27. 2.875

SKILLS PRACTICE 2

1. 50%
2. 75%
3. 62.5%

4. 80%
5. $\frac{2}{5}$
6. $\frac{1}{8}$

7. $\frac{1}{3}$
8. $\frac{5}{4}$
9. 48

10. 40.5
11. 93.75
12. 21.6

13. 24
14. 40
15. 100

16. 90
17. 160
18. 70

19. 225
20. 200
21. $\frac{2}{3}$

22. 90%
23. $33\frac{1}{3}$%
24. 80%

25. $66\frac{2}{3}$%
26. 120%

SKILLS PRACTICE 3

1. addition, subtraction, multiplication, division
2. to find a single number equivalent to a given expression
3. 96
4. 51
5. 107

6. 107
7. 55
8. 83

9. 36
10. 36
11. 1

12. 4
13. 28
14. 8

15. 28
16. $8\frac{4}{5}$
17. $8\frac{4}{5}$

18. 8
19. 48
20. 94

21. 0.875
22. 12.5%
23. 18

24. 12
25. $\frac{143}{6}$

SKILLS PRACTICE 4

1. $6 + d$
2. $6 - d$
3. $6d$

4. $\frac{6}{d}$
5. $7 + \frac{1}{2}x$
6. $7 + 2x$

7. a letter used in place of a number
8. to replace a variable with a number
9. to find a single number equivalent to the expression

10. a. 7 b. 6.5
11. a. 28 b. 20

12. a. $2\frac{1}{2}$ b. 5
13. $9 + 7$

14. $6 - 2$
15. $3 - x$
16. $x + y$

17. $1\frac{7}{12}$
18. $\frac{5}{8}$
19. $\frac{1}{12}$

20. $1\frac{1}{9}$
21. 12
22. 2

SKILLS PRACTICE 5

1. base   exponent   power
2. 8
3. 9
4. 32

5. 25
6. $\frac{9}{16}$

7. a. $3 \cdot 3 \cdot 3 \cdot 3$ b. 3^4
8. a. $2 \cdot 2 \cdot 2 \cdot 2 \cdot 2 \cdot 2$ b. 2^6
9. a. $4 \cdot 4 \cdot 4$ b. 4^3
10. a. $8 \cdot 8$ b. 8^2

11. 125
12. 49
13. 100,000

14. 27
15. 0.01
16. $34\frac{1}{2}$

17. $8\frac{3}{4}$
18. 36
19. 18

20. x^2

SKILLS PRACTICE 6

1. (1) remove groupings (2) evaluate powers (3) multiply and divide left to right (4) add or subtract left to right

2. 10   3. 40   4. 32

5. 24   6. 6   7. 7

8. 2   9. 77   10. 32

11. 11   12. a. 36   b. 0.04

13. a. 39   b. 3.04

14. a. 6   b. 12

15. a. 47   b. 117   c. 2.76

16. 32   17. 121.5   18. $1\frac{11}{12}$

19. 2.25   20. 160

SKILLS PRACTICE 7

1. $8 + y$ 2. $8 + y + 3$

3. $2(8 + y)$ 4. $\dfrac{8 + y}{2}$

5. $6x + 7$ 6. $\dfrac{5 + x}{3}$

7. $\dfrac{3}{5 + x}$ 8. $5y - 9$

9. $9 - 5y$ 10. $25 + x^2$

11. $(5 + x)^2$ 12. $6 + x - 8$

13. $8 - (6 + x)$ 14. $(y + x)^2$

15. $5 \cdot 4 \cdot x$ 16. $5(4 + x)$

17. $6y - 25$ 18. $(7 + x)8$

19. $7x + 8$ 20. $(6 - y) + (4 + y)$

21. 40.4   22. 34

23. $66\frac{2}{3}\%$ 24. $83\frac{1}{3}\%$

SKILLS PRACTICE 8

1. a. $x + 3 = 18$ b. $x = 15$

2. a. 29   b. $x = 45$

3. a. 192   b. 3   c. $2\frac{1}{4}$

4. $x = 7$ 5. $x = 39$ 6. $x = 145$

7. $x = 17$ 8. $x = 7$ 9. $x = 7\frac{1}{2}$

10. $x = 6\frac{3}{4}$ 11. $x = 432$ 12. $x = 97.6$

13. $x = 50$ 14. $x = 13.5$ 15. $x = 3\frac{1}{5}$

16. 9   17. 5   18. 87

19. 0.7834   20. 3, 6, 9, 12, 15, 18, 21

SKILLS PRACTICE 9

1. a. $2x + 16$ b. $8x$

2. a. distance around outside b. surface inside

3. a. $2x + 8$ b. 20 c. 20 d. $2x + 8 = 28$ e. $4x$ sq units f. 24 sq units g. 24 sq units h. 32 sq units i.$4x = 28$ j. $x = 7$ sq units k.$x = 14$ sq units

4. When you evaluate you know the value of the variable. When you solve, you find the value of the variable.

5. a. 22   b. 13

6. a. 22.5   b. 7.2

7. $58\frac{1}{12}$ 8. $\dfrac{41}{51}$ 9. $7 - 5x$

10. a. $2\frac{1}{2}$ b. $1\frac{5}{16}$

SKILLS PRACTICE 10

1. $x - 3$ 2. $d + 6.5$

3. a. x = # of ft in width b. $2x$ = # of ft in length c. 4 ft d. $2x = 12$ e. $x = 6$ f. evaluate the expression

4. a. x = # of ¢ Paul spends b. $x - 45$ = # of ¢ Stephanie spends c. 180¢, 270¢ d. 269¢, 192¢

5. 70%   6. 12.5%   7. 10.23 mi/hr

8. 57   9. $24.41\overline{6}$

SKILLS PRACTICE 11

1. 48   2. 37   3. $\dfrac{3}{2}$

4. $3\frac{1}{3}$ 5. 625,000 6. 0

7. 38   8. a. 24   b. 1.86

9. a. 40   b. 16   10. 7^3

11. b^5

Answers

12. **a.** $x + 8 - 3$ **b.** $(9 - y)^2$ **c.** $(x - 6) \cdot 5$
d. $4^3 + x^3$ **e.** $(4 + x)^3$ **f.** $3z + 17$

13. **a.** Let x = # of min for teacher to take test.
$2.3x$ = # of min for students **b.** 34.5 min,
48.3 min **c.** 24 min

SKILLS PRACTICE 12

1. 1, 2, 3, ...   2. $\frac{1}{2}, \frac{3}{4}$, 0.85,...

3. 0   4. $1 + 2 = 3$

5. $-1 + (-3) = -4$ 6. $2 + (-1) = 1$

7. $1 + (-3) = -2$, etc.

8. **a-e.** Check student work.

9. $(x + 3)^2$ 10. 70   11. $2\frac{11}{12}$

12. 28   13. 30

SKILLS PRACTICE 13

1. 4   2. -4 3. -28

4. $\frac{1}{4}$ 5. 0.25   6. 8

7. -36 8. -33 9. -33

10. -145 11. -59 12. 0

13. 0   14. -16 15. 17

16. 12   17. 3   18. 6

19. -17 20. -4 21. 4

22. 20   23. 68

24. **a.** $4x$ **b.** 6.5   **c.** solve

25. **a.** $x = 28$ **b.** $x = 6$

26. $2 + x$ Answers may vary.

SKILLS PRACTICE 14

1. 3   2. -3 3. -13

4. -3 5. 13   6. -3

7. 99   8. -51 9. -15

10. 22   11. -17 12. 35

13. 0   14. 0   15. 5

16. -4.6 17. 4.6   18. $-6\frac{1}{4}$

19. 81

20. **a.** 18 **b.** 28 **c.** 8 **d.** 38

21. 4   22. 4   23. -17

24. 87.5%   25. 90   26. 5.6

27. 10,004,037.45   28. $2^3 \cdot 3^2$

SKILLS PRACTICE 15

1. -8 2. 8   3. -8

4. -8 5. -8 6. 81

7. -81 8. 120   9. -120

10. -432 11. 24   12. -108

13. **a.** -2 **b.** 4 **c.** -8 **d.** 16 **e.** -32

14. **a. i.** -4 **ii.** 4 **b. i.** -4 **ii.** 4

15. **a.** 36 **b.** -36 **c.** 36 **d.** -36 **e.** -13 **f.** 5
g. -5 **h.** -5

16. $x^2 + y^2$ 17. $9x - 8$

18. $\dfrac{6 + x}{5y}$ 19. 16

SKILLS PRACTICE 16

1. $2; -\frac{1}{2}$ 2. $\frac{x}{y} = x \cdot \frac{1}{y}; y \neq 0$

3. $4; 5; \frac{2}{3}; -\frac{3}{2}; -8; -\frac{1}{8}; -\frac{1}{6}; \frac{1}{6}; 0$

4. -2 5. 2   6. -9

7. 3   8. -4 9. 2

10. 6   11. 0   12. 0

13. not defined 14. not defined 15. $1\frac{4}{5}$

16. **a.** -2 **b.** 0 **c.** not defined

17. **a.** -1 **b.** not defined **c.** -1

18. **a.** -5 **b.** 5 **c.** not defined

19. **a.** -16 **b.** $5\frac{1}{3}$

20. **a.** -2 **b.** 2 **c.** not defined

21. $x = 11$ 22. $x = 6$ 23. $x = 12$

SKILLS PRACTICE 17

1. 9   2. 26   3. 23

4. -20 5. -2 6. 15

7. 38   8. $-12\frac{1}{2}$ 9. 42

10. -21 11. -183 12. 4

13. 22   14. –3   15. –2

16. **a.** 4 **b.** 1 **c.** not defined **d.** 0

17. **a.** 38 **b.** 70

18. $x = -6$ 19. $x = 2$ 20. $x = -7$

21. $x = -18$ 22. $x = -14$ 23. $x = 5\frac{3}{4}$

24. $x = 5$

SKILLS PRACTICE 18

1. $y + 11$ 2. $x - 2$ 3. $y + 2$

4. $3x - 20$ 5. $-x + 5$ 6. $-2x + 17$

7. $-5x - 10$ 8. $10x$ 9. $-32y$

10. $-24x$ 11. $20x$ 12. $-56x$

13. $32x$ 14. $6x$ 15. $-6x$

16. $-2x$ 17. $6x$ 18. $-28x$

19. x 20. $4x$

21. **a.** 11 **b.** 3   22. 2^6

23. $8x + 3$ 24. 2   25. 4

SKILLS PRACTICE 19

1. $x = 3$ 2. $x = 4$ 3. $x = -4$

4. $x = 6$ 5. $x = 3$ 6. $x = -10$

7. $x = 9$ 8. $x = -2\frac{1}{4}$ 9. $x = -16\frac{1}{5}$

10. $x = 3$ 11. $4 = x$ 12. $x = 15$

13. $x = -9$ 14. $x = -1$ 15. $x = -5$

16. $x = 4\frac{1}{3}$ 17. $x = -7$ 18. $x = 18$

19. $x = 17$ 20. $x = -3$ 21. $3x - 8$

22. $8 - 3x$ 23. $2^3 \cdot 3$

24. **a.** –4 **b.** 14

25. **a.** not defined **b.** –1

SKILLS PRACTICE 20

1. **a.** 33 **b.** $4x + 5 = 37$ **c.** 8 **d.** $4(12) + 5 = 53$ No, because it would take him 53 minutes to do 12 problems.

2. **a.** $545 - 45b = $ # of ¢ left after b bags **b.** 8 **c.** Wrote an equation and solved **d.** 5¢ or $0.05 **e.** $545 - 45(15) = -130$ No. After 15 bags he would have –1.30 dollars remaining which is less than 0.

3. 25   4. $-2\frac{5}{6}$ 5. –17.5

6. –490

SKILLS PRACTICE 21

1. 9   2. 14   3. –48

4. 1   5. 2   6. –24

7. –93   8. –3   9. 13

10. $5\frac{1}{3}$ 11. 8   12. 8

13. 0   14. –6

15. **a.** 2 **b.** 12

16. **a.** not defined **b.** 0

17. $x - 5$ 18. $-x + 13$ 19. $45x$

20. $6x$ 21. $x = -2$ 22. $x = -6$

23. $x = -2$ 24. $x = 5$

25. **a. i.** $m = $ # of miles she rides **ii.** $4m = $ # of miles ridden **iii.** $4m + 6 = $ total number of minute a ride will take **b.** 50 min **c.** 24 mi **d.** 15 mph

SKILLS PRACTICE 22

1. $3x + 18$ 2. $5x - 40$ 3. $-6x + 30$

4. $-3x - 9$ 5. $x^2 + 2x$ 6. $2x^2 + 4x$

7. $2x - 6$ 8. $6x + 2$ 9. $-6x + 4\frac{1}{2}$

10. $-2x - \frac{4}{9}$ 11. $2x + 13$ 12. $3x - 7$

13. $31 - 4x$ 14. $40x - 28$

15. $-2x + 23$ 16. $-5x + 26$

17. $6x + 3$ 18. $-8x - 22$

19. $22 - 5x$ 20. $30x + 39$

21. $x = 6\frac{1}{2}$ 22. $x = 26$

23. $x = 1$ 24. $x = 0$ 25. $x = -2$

SKILLS PRACTICE 23

1. $6x + 8$ 2. $6x - 8$ 3. $-7 - x$

4. $-7 + x$ 5. $2x + 3$ 6. $2x + 3$

7. $56x - 35$ **8.** $-18 + 24x$ **9.** $-3x + 2$

10. $3x - 3y + 21$ **11.** $-6x + 12y + 18$

12. $-6x + 12y + 18$ **13.** $-8 + x$

14. $-x + 8$ **15.** $-6x + 5$

16. $-6x + 5$ **17.** $32 - 24x$

18. $8 + 12x - 10y$ **19.** $-4x + 3y - 4\frac{1}{2}$

20. $4 + 6x$ **21.** $-6x + 8$ **22.** $5x - 17$

23. $-x + 3$ **24.** $4y - 3$ **25.** $7x + 7$

SKILLS PRACTICE 24

1. $5x$ **2.** $-3x$ **3.** $5x$

4. $-8x$ **5.** $6x - 2$ **6.** $6x$

7. $5 + 3x$ **8.** $-5x + 13$ **9.** $x + 10$

10. $2x - 7$ **11.** $-14x + 2$ **12.** $14 - 14x$

13. $1 - 3x$ **14.** $1 - 3x$ **15.** $11 - 12x$

16. $-20x - 18$ **17.** $x + 2$

18. $17 + 6x$ **19.** $17 + 6x$ **20.** $2 - 17x$

21. $x - 35$ **22.** $\frac{3}{4}y$ **23.** $2s$

24. **a.** -14 **b.** 10 **25.** **a.** 19 **b.** 7

SKILLS PRACTICE 25

1. $7 - x$ **2.** $7x + 15$

3. $-4x^2 - 24x - 4$ **4.** $-6x^2 + 29x + 15$

5. $5x - 1$ **6.** $6x^2 - 26x + 17$

7. $10x^2 + 4x - 2$ **8.** $5x^2 + 16x - 13$

9. $20x^2 - 20x - 15$ **10.** $-x^2 + 16x + 8$

11. $x^3 + y^3 + 4x^2 + x + 9$

12. $-4x - 48$ **13.** $-x^2 + 17x$

14. $-12x + 30$ **15.** $-8 + 4x$

16. $-3xy + 10x$ **17.** $xy + 8y - 32$

18. $9x^2 + 30x + 25$ **19.** $x^2 - 25$

20. $25x^2 - 4$

SKILLS PRACTICE 26

1. commutative addition **2.** symmetric **3.** additive inverse **4.** additive identity **5.** definition of subtraction **6.** associative addition **7.** commutative multiplication **8.** transitive **9.** distributive **10.** multiplicative identity **11.** multiplicative inverse **12.** definition of division **13.** commutative multiplication **14.** definition of subtraction **15.** distributive **16.** associative multiplication **17.** reflexive **18.** commutative addition **19.** associative addition **20.** distributive

21. $8x$ **22.** $3 + 5x$ **23.** $5x - 9$

24. $3x - 7$ **25.** $3x + 9$ **26.** $30x$

SKILLS PRACTICE 27

1. **a.** commutative addition **b.** associative addition **c.** arithmetic

2. **a.** distributive **b.** arithmetic **c.** commutative addition **d.** associative addition **e.** arithmetic

3. **a.** multiplicative property of -1 **b.** distributive **c.** multiplicative property of -1 **d.** associative addition **e.** arithmetic **f.** definition of subtraction

4. **a.** definition of subtraction **b.** commutative addition **c.** associative addition **d.** arithmetic **e.** definition of subtraction **f.** distributive **g.** arithmetic **h.** commutative addition

5. **a.** additive property of equality **b.** associative addition **c.** additive inverse **d.** additive identity **e.** arithmetic

6. **a.** multiplicative property of equality **b.** associative multiplication **c.** multiplicative inverse **d.** multiplicative identity **e.** arithmetic

SKILLS PRACTICE 28

1. $5x - 15$ **2.** $-x + 2$ **3.** $-16 + 8x$

4. $6x + 15$ **5.** $1 + x$ **6.** $7x - 13$

7. $-1 + 8x$ **8.** $4x + 5$ **9.** $16x - 9$

10. $23x - 26$ **11.** $2(x + 2)$

12. $3(2 - x)$ **13.** $2(x + y)$

14. $4(2x - 3)$ **15.** $3(1 - 2x + 3y)$

16. **a.** distributivity **b.** arithmetic **c.** definition of subtraction **d.** commutative addition **e.** associative addition **f.** arithmetic **g.** distributive **h.** arithmetic

17. **a.** additive property of equality
b. associative addition **c.** arithmetic
d. additive inverse **e.** additive identity

18. **a.** multiplicative property of equality
b. associtive multiplication
c. multiplicative inverse **d.** multiplicative
identity **e.** definition of division
f. arithmetic

SKILLS PRACTICE 29

1. $x = 3$　　2. $x = 7$　　3. $x = 2$

4. $x = -4$　　5. $x = -3$　　6. $x = 5$

7. $x = \frac{1}{10}$　　8. $x = 1$　　9. $x = 0$

10. $x = -4$　　11. commutative addition

12. definition of subtraction

13. commutative addition

14. symmetric　　15. distributive

16. **a.** not defined　**b.** 0　**c.** $-2\frac{1}{2}$

SKILLS PRACTICE 30

1. $x = -3$　　2. $x = -1\frac{4}{5}$　3. $x = 6$

4. $x = 3$　　5. $x = 1$　　6. $x = \frac{1}{2}$

7. $x = 1$　　8. $x = -5$　　9. $x = -1$

10. $x = -20$　11. $x = -20$　12. $x = 7$

13. $x = 7$　　14. $x = 6$　　15. $x = 0$

16. $x = 2$　　17. $x = 1\frac{1}{3}$　18. $x = 5$

19. $x = 8$　　20. $x = 11$　21. **a.** 6 **b.** 26

22. **a.** 8 **b.** 12　　23. **a.** 0 **b.** 80

24. -1　　　　25. 1

SKILLS PRACTICE 31

1. $x = -6$　　2. $x = -2$　　3. $x = 2$

4. $x = 1$　　5. $x = 4$　　6. $x = 1$

7. $x = -9$　　8. $x = 3$　　9. $x = 0$

10. $x = 0$　　11. $x = 5$　　12. $x = 2$

13. $x = -3\frac{1}{2}$　14. $x = 5\frac{4}{5}$　15. $x = 5$

16. $x = -3$　17. Ø　　　18. all reals

19. $x = 0$　　20. $x = 0$　　21. Ø

22. $x = 1\frac{1}{2}$　23. $\frac{3}{5}$　　　24. $-\frac{5}{3}$

25. no number • 0 = 1

26. **a.** -19　**b.** $x = -4$　**c.** $x = 12$

27. $24 - 6x$

SKILLS PRACTICE 32

1. $x = -6.17$　2. $x = 5$　　3. $x = 1.59$

4. $x = -5.32$　5. $x = 0.53$　6. $x = 0.41$

7. $x = 1.82$　8. $x = -0.41$　9. $x = -0.09$

10. Ø　　　11. $6x + 25$　12. $76 - 6d$

13. $24 - 2.5f$　14. $426 + 12x$ (2.50)

15. $5800

SKILLS PRACTICE 33

1. **a. i.** $72 - 8m$ **ii.** $50 - 6m$

   b. i. $72 - 8m = 50 - 6m$ **ii.** They won't
   have the same # of cookies until 9 minutes
   later when they both have 0. **c.** Javier: 64,
   56, 8; John: 44, 38, 2 **d.** about 5.14 min
   e. John. It took him 8.3 min. It would have
   taken Javier 9 min.

2. **a. i.** $18h$ **ii.** $235 - 18h$ **iii.** $28h$
   iv. $358 - 28h$ **b.** Sam; 63 pages **c.** $358 - 28h = 0$; 12.79 hours **d.** $235 - 18h = 358 - 28h$; $h = 12.3$ hours **e.** Sam; 4.78 pages

SKILLS PRACTICE 34

1. $x = -72$　2. $x = 9$　　3. $x = 11$

4. $x = 11$　　5. $x = -6$　　6. $x = -24$

7. $x = -8$　　8. $x = 0$　　9. Ø

10. all real numbers　　11. $x = -94.17$

12. **a. i.** $0.25x$ **ii.** $x - 5$ **iii.** $0.3(x - 5)$
    b. i. Jay; 1.1 mi **ii.** Bill; 0.3 mi **c.** 30
    min **d.** Bill; Jay will take 11 more minutes.

13. **a. i.** $45x$ **ii.** $36x + 90$ **b.** Olivia 225;
    Chad 270 **c.** 10 min

SKILLS PRACTICE 35

1. $2x^3 + 3x^2 - 5$

2. $-3x^5 + 5x^4 + 4x^3 + 18$

3. $-x^5 + x^4 - x^3 + x^2$

4. $-5x^4 + 4x^3 + 6x^2 + 18x - 24$

5. $-7x^4 - 5x^3 + 6x^2 + 4x + 8$

6. $5 \cdot x \cdot x \cdot y \cdot y \cdot y$

7. 26 8. definition of subtraction

9. commutative addition 10. transitive

11. distributive 12. associative multiplication

SKILLS PRACTICE 36

1. yes 2. yes
3. no, absolute value of a variable 4. yes
5. no, division by a variable
6. quadratic monomial 7. linear binomial
8. quadratic trinomial 9. cubic with 4 term
10. quadratic binomial 11. linear monomial
12. cubic binomial 13. quadratic trinomial
14. linear binomial
15. 5, –4, 1 16. x^2, etc. 17. $x + 1$, etc.

18. $x^2 + x + 1$ 19. $x^3 + x^2 + x + 1$

20. a. $x + 2$, etc.   b. $\frac{2}{x}$, etc.

21. $8x^2 + 2x$ 22. $4x + 2$

23. $5x^3 + 6x$ 24. $-2x^2 - 4x + 6$

25. $x^2 - 9x + 20$

SKILLS PRACTICE 37

1. $x^2 + 7x + 12$ 2. $x^2 - 9x + 20$

3. $x^2 + 3x - 4$ 4. $x^2 - 3x - 10$

5. $x^2 - 3x - 10$ 6. $x^2 - 2x - 15$

7. $15x^2 - 26x + 8$ 8. $2x^2 + 8x - 42$

9. $-15x^2 - 2x + 8$ 10. $25x^2 + 30x + 9$

11. $x^2 - 81$ 12. $4x^2 - 12x + 9$

13. $4x^2 - 9$ 14. $x^2 + 10x + 25$

15. $36x^2 + 48x + 7$ 16. $4x^2 - 12x + 9$

17. $25x^2 + 30x + 9$ 18. $x^2 + 10x + 25$

19. $3x^2 - 3$ 20. $6x^2 + 9x - 6$

21. $-x^2 + 16$ 22. $4x^2 + 28x + 49$

23. $12x^2 + x - 20$ 24. $9x^2 - 9x + 2$

25. $56x^2 - 19x - 15$ 26. $x = -4$

27. all real numbers 28. $x = 0$

29. $x = -5.\overline{4}$ or $-5\frac{4}{9}$ 30. $x = \frac{1}{4}$

SKILLS PRACTICE 38

1. $(x + 3)(x + 4)$ 2. $(x + 6)(x + 2)$

3. $(x + 12)(x + 1)$ 4. $(x - 2)(x - 3)$

5. $(x - 4)(x - 1)$ 6. $(x + 4)(x + 2)$

7. $(x - 2)(x - 4)$ 8. $(x + 4)(x + 4)$

9. $(x - 4)(x - 4)$ 10. $(x - 8)(x - 2)$

11. $(x + 6)(x + 4)$ 12. $(x - 8)(x - 3)$

13. $(x + 3)(x + 3)$ 14. $(x - 5)(x - 5)$

15. prime   16. $(x - 2)(x - 9)$

17. prime   18. $(x - 1)(x - 1)$

19. $(x + 2)(x + 2)$ 20. $(x - 5)(x - 4)$

21. $2x^2 - 5x - 12$ 22. $4x^2 - 2x - 12$

23. $x^2 + 10x + 25$ 24. $9x^2 - 4$

25. $9x^2 + 24x + 16$

SKILLS PRACTICE 39

1. $(x - 3)(x + 2)$ 2. $(x + 3)(x - 2)$

3. $(x + 6)(x - 2)$ 4. $(x + 4)(x - 3)$

5. $(x + 12)(x - 1)$ 6. $(x - 6)(x + 4)$

7. $(x - 6)(x + 5)$ 8. $(x + 9)(x - 5)$

9. $(x - 6)(x + 2)$ 10. $(x - 2)(x + 1)$

11. prime   12. $(x - 4)(x + 1)$

13. $(x + 5)(x - 1)$ 14. prime

15. $(x - 5)(x + 2)$ 16. $(x - 5)(x + 5)$

17. $(x - 6)(x - 2)$ 18. $(x + 3)(x + 6)$

19. $(x - 1)(x + 1)$ 20. $(x - 1)(x - 1)$

21. x = time they both worked

$2(x + 6) + 2x = 50$ $x = 9\frac{1}{2}$ min

22. quadratic binomial

23. quadratic trinomial

24. cubic trinomial   **25.** linear binomial

SKILLS PRACTICE 40

1. $(2x + 1)(x + 2)$ **2.** $(2x + 1)(x + 3)$

3. $(2x + 3)(x - 1)$ **4.** $(2x - 1)(x + 3)$

5. $(2x - 1)(x - 3)$ **6.** $(3x - 1)(x - 4)$

7. $(3x - 2)(x - 2)$ **8.** $(2x - 3)(2x + 1)$

9. $(2x + 3)(x - 5)$ **10.** $(5x + 1)(5x - 3)$

11. $(3x - 1)(3x + 1)$ **12.** $(2x - 5)(2x - 5)$

13. prime   **14.** $(3x + 1)(2x - 1)$

15. prime   **16.** $(3x - 2)(2x + 3)$

17. $(3x - 1)(x - 3)$ **18.** $(2x + 1)(x - 2)$

19. $(4x - 5)(x + 1)$ **20.** prime

21. $6x^2 + 2x - 4$ **22.** $4x^2 + 4x + 1$

23. $x^2 - 25$ **24.** $2x^2 + 15x - 27$

25. $x^2 - 2x + 1$

SKILLS PRACTICE 41

1. $(x - 2)(x + 2)$ **2.** $(x - 3)(x + 3)$

3. $(x - 4)(x + 4)$ **4.** $(x - 5)(x + 5)$

5. $(2x + 1)(2x - 1)$ **6.** $(3x - 1)(3x + 1)$

7. $(2x + 3)(2x - 3)$ **8.** $(3x - 7)(3x + 7)$

9. $(1 - 2x)(1 + 2x)$ **10.** $(5 - 6x)(5 + 6x)$

11. $(x - 1)(x + 1)$ **12.** prime

13. $(x - 5)(x + 5)$ **14.** prime

15. $(x - 9)(x + 9)$ **16.** prime

17. $(2 - x)(2 + x)$ **18.** $(3 - 5x)(3 + 5x)$

19. prime   **20.** $(x - y)(x + y)$

21. $(x + 3)(x + 2)$ **22.** $(3x + 1)(x + 1)$

23. $(4x + 1)(x - 1)$ **24.** $(x - 2)(x - 2)$

25. $(x - 1)(x - 1)$

SKILLS PRACTICE 42

1. $x^2 + 4x + 4$ **2.** $x^2 - 6x + 9$

3. $x^2 + 2x + 1$ **4.** $4x^2 + 4x + 1$

5. $9x^2 - 6x + 1$ **6.** $25x^2 + 20x + 4$

7. $1 + 6x + 9x^2$ **8.** $16x^2 - 8x + 1$

9. $25 - 30x + 9x^2$ **10.** $4x^2 - 12x + 9$

11. $4x^2 - 12x + 9$ **12.** $16x^2 - 40x + 25$

13. $x^2 + 2xy + y^2$ **14.** $x^2 - 4xy + 4y^2$

15. $9x^2 - 6xy + y^2$ **16.** $9x^2 + 12xy + 4y^2$

17. $25x^2 + 40x + 16$ **18.** $16x^2 + 40x + 25$

19. $x^2 - 2x + 1$ **20.** $1 - 2x + x^2$

21. $(x - 1)(x + 1)$ **22.** prime

23. $(x + 1)(x + 2)$ **24.** $(x - 4)(x + 1)$

25. prime

SKILLS PRACTICE 43

1. $(x + 2)^2$ **2.** $(x + 1)^2$ **3.** $(x + 3)^2$

4. $(x - 5)^2$ **5.** $(x - 6)^2$ **6.** $(x - 7)^2$

7. Cannot. -1 is not positive.

8. Cannot. -64 is not positive.

9. Cannot. 8 is not a perfect square.

10. $(x - 4)^2$ **11.** Cannot. 1 should be 4.

12. Cannot. -9 is not positive.

13. $(x - 12)^2$ **14.** $(x + 25)^2$ **15.** $(x + 14)^2$

16. Cannot. $9x$ should be $18x$.

17. Cannot. There is no middle term.

18. Cannot. $-30x$ should be $-50x$

19. $(2x + 1)^2$ **20.** $(3x - 1)^2$ **21.** $6x^2 - 7x - 3$

22. $4x^2 - 4x + 1$ **23.** $-x^2 - 2x + 3$

24. a. 7   **b.** 1   **25.** $x - \dfrac{3}{2}$

SKILLS PRACTICE 44

1. $(x + 3)(x + 4)$ **2.** $(x - 3)(x - 4)$

3. $(x - 4)(x + 3)$ **4.** $(x + 6)(x - 2)$

5. $(x - 6)(x + 2)$ **6.** $(5x + 1)(x + 1)$

7. $(3x - 1)(x + 1)$ **8.** $(2x + 1)(x + 3)$

9. $(2x + 1)(x + 2)$ **10.** $(2x - 1)(2x - 3)$

11. $(x - 6)(x + 6)$ **12.** $(x - 8)(x + 8)$

13. $(2x - 3)(x + 4)$ **14.** $(x - 4)^2$

15. prime   **16.** $(x + 5)^2$

17. $(x + 1)^2$ **18.** $(x - 1)^2$

19. $(x - 1)(x + 1)$ **20.** prime

21. $(x + 3)^2$ 22. $(x + 8)(x + 2)$

23. $(x + 8)(x - 2)$ 24. prime

25. $(x - 10)(x + 5)$ 26. $4x^2 - 18x + 34$

27. $6x^2 - 13x - 5$ 28. $9x^2 + 6x + 1$

29. 0.008   30. $11\frac{53}{60}$

31. 13.5   32. 1, 2, 3, 4, 6, 12

SKILLS PRACTICE 45

1. **a.** yes   **b.** yes   **c.** no

2. **a.** yes   **b.** no   **c.** yes   **d.** no

3. **a.** yes   **b.** no   **c.** yes   **d.** no

4. **a.** no   **b.** no

5. **a.** yes   **b.** no   **c.** yes   **d.** yes

6. **a.** 0, 1, $\frac{1}{2}$, etc.   **b.** –1, 0, 1, 2, etc.

   c. $\sqrt{2}$, $\sqrt{3}$, $\sqrt{5}$, etc.

   d. $-\sqrt{2}$ **e.** $\sqrt{-1}$

7. Rational. It can be written as a ratio of 314 over 100.

8. $x = -11$ 9. **a.** –9   **b.** –16

10. $x^2 + 2x + 1$ 11. 3^4

12. $0.41\overline{6}$ 13. 8:45 p.m.

SKILLS PRACTICE 46

1. **a.** $x + 2$ **b.** $\sqrt{x + 2}$

2. quadratic trinomial   3. linear binomial

4. quadratic monomial

5. cubic polynomial with four terms

6. $x^2 + x - 6$ 7. $6x^2 + 11x + 3$

8. $16x^2 - 8x + 1$ 9. $36x^2 - 1$

10. $12x^2 - 11x - 15$ 11. $x^2 + 2x + 1$

12. $x^2 - 2x + 1$ 13. $x^2 - 1$

14. $7x^2 + 26x - 8$ 15. $9x^2 - 12x + 4$

16. $(x + 3)(x - 2)$ 17. $(2x + 1)(x - 4)$

18. $(5x + 1)(5x - 3)$ 19. $(x - 2)(x - 3)$

20. $(x - 3)^2$ 21. prime

22. $(x + 1)(x - 1)$ 23. $(x - 1)^2$

24. prime   25. $(3x - 4)(3x + 4)$

26. $(2x - 1)(2x + 3)$ 27. $(x + 10)(x - 1)$

28. prime   29. $(3x - 1)(2x + 1)$

30. $(4x - 1)(x - 5)$ 31. $(x + 5)^2$

32. $(x - 5)(x + 5)$ 33. $(x - 2)^2$

34. $(x - 2)(x + 2)$ 35. $(x + 2)(x - 1)$

36. **a.** rational   **b.** rational

   c. rational   **d.** irrational

SKILLS PRACTICE 47

1. 6; rational   2. 2.5; rational

3. 7.91; irrational   4. 25; rational

5. 10.95; irrational   6. 17; rational

7. –8.66; irrational   8. –1.7; rational

9. 3   10. 1   11. 20

12. 20   13. 7.83   14. –6.17

15. 21   16. 15.81   17. 1.12

18. 0.87   19. 0.82   20. not real

21. $(x - 2)(x + 2)$ 22. $(x - 2)^2$

23. $(x - 2)(x + 1)$ 24. $(2x + 1)(x - 2)$

25. $(3x + 1)(x - 2)$

SKILLS PRACTICE 48

1. $|n| = n$ if $n \geq 0$; $|n| = -n$ if $n < 0$

2. 3   3. 4   4. **a.** 13 **b.** 3

5. **a.** 13 **b.** 19   6. **a.** 3 **b.** 13

7. $\{\pm 8\}$ 8. $\{\pm 7\}$ 9. $\emptyset$

10. $\{-11, 5\}$ 11. $\{-17, 7\}$ 12. $\{15, -3\}$

13. $\emptyset$ 14. $\{-3, 13\}$ 15. $\{-4, 20\}$

16. $\{-1, 4\}$ 17. $\{-4\frac{2}{3}, 2\}$ 18. $\{-6, 0\}$

19. $\{0, -8\}$ 20. $\{-4\}$ 21. $(x - 4)(x - 3)$

22. $(x - 6)(x + 2)$ 23. $(x - 4)(x + 3)$

24. prime   25. $(x + 1)^2$

SKILLS PRACTICE 49

1. $\{\pm 8\}$ 2. $\{\pm 5.29\}$ 3. $\varnothing$

4. $\{-3, 1\}$ 5. $\{-3, -1\}$ 6. $\{-7, 1\}$

7. $\varnothing$ 8. $\{0.84, 7.16\}$

9. $\{-15, 1\}$ 10. $\{5.17, 10.83\}$

11. $\{1\}$ 12. $\{-3, 2\}$ 13. $\{-1.74, 2.74\}$

14. $\{3.\overline{6}, -1\}$ 15. $\{-1.31, 0.81\}$

16. $\{\pm 1\}$ 17. $\{\pm 1.30\}$ 18. $\{-7, 13\}$

19. $\{-1.57, 2.90\}$ 20. $\varnothing$

21. $\{\pm 25\}$ 22. $\{\pm 5\}$ 23. $\{-20, 30\}$

24. $\{-20, 30\}$ 25. $\varnothing$

SKILLS PRACTICE 50

1. $\{-3, 1\}$ 2. $\{-7, 1\}$ 3. $\{-5, 9\}$

4. $\{-1, 11\}$ 5. $\{-0.16, 6.16\}$

6. $\{0, 14\}$ 7. $\{-24, 4\}$ 8. $\{-8.47, 0.47\}$

9. $\{-1.14, 3.34\}$ 10. $\{-3.40, 19.40\}$

11. $\{-12.5, 3.5\}$ 12. $\varnothing$

13. $\{2\}$ 14. $\{-1.5, 0.5\}$

15. $\{-2.82, 9.82\}$ 16. $\{0.17, 5.83\}$

17. $\{0.05, 21.95\}$ 18. $\{0, -24\}$

19. $\varnothing$ 20. $\{-4, 1\}$ 21. $\{-26, 23\}$

22. $\{-5, 2\}$ 23. $\{23\}$ 24. $\{21.5\}$

25. $\{3\}$

SKILLS PRACTICE 51

1. $x^2 - 12x + 36$ 2. $x^2 + 2x + 1$

3. $x^2 + 6x + 9$ 4. $x^2 - 10x + 25$

5. $x^2 + 14x + 49$ 6. $x^2 - 4x + 4$

7. $1, (x + 1)^2$ 8. $1, (x - 1)^2$

9. $9, (x - 3)^2$ 10. $16, (x + 4)^2$

11. $25, (x - 5)^2$ 12. $4, (x + 2)^2$

13. $36, (x + 6)^2$ 14. $0.25, (x + 0.5)^2$

15. $49, (x - 7)^2$ 16. $20.25, (x + 4.5)^2$

17. $324, (x + 18)^2$ 18. $64, (x + 8)^2$

19. $1024, (x - 32)^2$ 20. $0.25, (x - 0.5)^2$

21. $\{-7, 1\}$ 22. $\{-9, -1\}$ 23. $\{13.6, -12\}$

24. $\varnothing$ 25. $\{14\}$

SKILLS PRACTICE 52

1. $\{-5, -1\}$ 2. $\{2, 4\}$ 3. $\{-3, -1\}$

4. $\{9, -1\}$ 5. $\{5, -1\}$ 6. $\{-4, 2\}$

7. $\{-3, 1\}$ 8. $\{-8.87, -1.13\}$

9. $\{-4, 1\}$ 10. $\{2, 3\}$ 11. $\{3, 4\}$

12. $\{2, -1\}$ 13. $\{-5.70, 0.70\}$

14. $\{1.30, 7.70\}$ 15. $\{3, 1\}$

16. $\{-1\}$ 17. $\varnothing$ 18. $\varnothing$

19. $\{-1.04, 4.04\}$ 20. $\varnothing$

21. $\{\pm 5\}$ 22. $\{\pm 7\}$ 23. $\{31, -41\}$

24. $\{1, -11\}$ 25. $\{-5, 11\}$

SKILLS PRACTICE 53

1. $a = 2; b = -1; c = 7$

2. $a = 1; b = 5; c = -8$

3. $a = 5; b = 6; c = -12$

4. $a = 3; b = -9; c = -13$

5. $\{-1, -3\}$ 6. $\{1, 3\}$ 7. $\{-1, 6\}$

8. $\{3, 2\}$ 9. $\{-3, -0.5\}$

10. $\{-4, 1.5\}$ 11. $\{-1, -0.\overline{3}\}$

12. $\{-3\}$ 13. $\{-8, -2\}$

14. $\varnothing$ 15. $\{1\}$

16. $\{-2.17, 0.92\}$ 17. $\{-0.36, 0.56\}$

18. $\{-1.45, 3.45\}$ 19. $\varnothing$

20. $\{2.48, -0.81\}$ 21. $\{2, 4\}$

22. $\{1.71, -11.71\}$ 23. $\{25, -20\}$

24. $\{25\}$ 25. $\{-9, 5\}$

SKILLS PRACTICE 54

1. a. $d = 10t - 5t^2$ b. i. 5 m ii. 3.75 m
iii. 3.75 m c. after 2 seconds d. After 1
second it went 5 m e. No, maximum height
was 5 m

2. a. i. 3 m ii. 2.75 m iii. 0.75 m
b. On the way up since it was higher
after 1 s
c. i. 1.4 m   ii. 4.4 m   d. 1.9 s
e. No, the equation has no solution.

SKILLS PRACTICE 55

1. 45: real, irrational; – 6: none; 36: real, rational; 0: real, rational; 8: real, irrational

2. $D = -7$; not real   3. $D = 9$; real, rat.

4. $D = 68$; real, irr.   5. $D = 13$; real, irr.

6. $D = 1$; real, rat.   7. $D = 13$; real, irr.

8. $D = -8$; not real   9. $D = 120$; real, irr.

10. $D = 25$; real, rat.   11. $D = 64$; real, rat.

12. $D = 36$; real, rat.   13. $D = 25$; real, rat.

14. $D = -75$; not real   15. $D = 16$; real, rat.

16. $D = 21$; real, irr.   17. $D = 28$; real, irr.

18. $D = 4$; real, rat.   19. $D = 0$; real, rat.

20. $D = 9$; real, rat.   21. $x = 2.5$

22. $x = 3$ 23. $x = \dfrac{1}{3}$ or $x = 3$

24. $\varnothing$ 25. $x = 3.\overline{3}$ or $x = 3\dfrac{1}{3}$

SKILLS PRACTICE 56

1. $\{-3, 15\}$ 2. $\{-8.5, 8\}$ 3. $\varnothing$

4. $\{15, 1\}$ 5. $\{-8, 2\}$ 6. $\{-2.\overline{3}, 3\}$

7. $\{-4, 8\}$ 8. $\{-3.24, 1.24\}$

9. $\{-9, 1\}$ 10. $\{4, 1\}$ 11. $\{-5.16, 1.16\}$

12. $\{-4, -3\}$ 13. $\{0.5, 1\}$ 14. $\{-2.52, 1.19\}$

15. $\varnothing$ 16. $\{6, 2\}$

17. (12) $D = 1$; rational; (13) $D = 1$; rational; (14) $D = 124$; irrational; (15) $D = -15$, not real; (16) $D = 16$; rational

18. a. $d = 16t - 5t^2$ b. after 2 s and 1.2 s
   c. 12 m; it was on the way down because at 1.2 s the ball was also at 12 m.
   d. 3 m
   e. 3.2 s

SKILLS PRACTICE 57

1. $21x - 98$ 2. $4x^2 - 12x + 9$

3. $2x^2 + 3x - 20$ 4. $-16x + 70$

5. $-10y$ 6. $-3x^2 - 16x + 23$

7. $3x^2 + 4.5x - 6$ 8. 18

9. a. -35 b. 49   10. a. $18\dfrac{3}{4}$ b. 0.03

11. a. 18 b. 22   12. a. 6 b. 110

13. a. $\dfrac{1}{2}$ b. -8

14. commutative addition

15. mult. prop. of -1 16. symmetric

17. distributive   18. associative mult.

19. $(x - 5)(x + 5)$ 20. $(x - 2)(x - 4)$

21. $(x - 4)(x + 3)$ 22. $(3x - 2)(x + 1)$

23. $x = 4$ 24. $x = 11.5$

25. $x = 0.4$ 26. $x = 2$

SKILLS PRACTICE 58

1. a. 25 b. -10 c. 13 d. -3.4

2. a. 51 b. -40 c. 25.6

3. a. 40 b. 9 c. 1.36 d. 1.5

4. a. 2 b. -28 c. $-\dfrac{2}{9}$

5. a. -8 b. 17 c. 46

6. a. 16 b. 16   7 a. 16 b. 16

8. $x^2 + 8x + 16$ 9. $(x - 8)(x + 2)$

10. $(3x + 1)(x + 2)$ 11. $(3x + 1)(x - 2)$

12. $\{22\}$ 13. $\{2, -8\}$

SKILLS PRACTICE 59

1-9. Check student plots.

10. a. 1 b. 2 c. 4 d. 3 e. 5 f. 5, 6, 9 g. 5, 7, 8

11. a-b. Check student graphs. c. -3.4 d. 2.7

12. $\{2\}$ 13. a. 21 b. $x = \dfrac{3 \pm \sqrt{33}}{4}$

14. Answers may vary. $ax^2 + bx + c$

15. a. 11 b. 5 c. $x = \dfrac{1}{2}, -3\dfrac{1}{2}$ d. $\varnothing$

SKILLS PRACTICE 60

1-2. Check student graphs.

3. #1 slants up, #2 slants down; #1 is uphill.

4. 2

5. $y = -3x + 1$

6. $y = 2x - 4$

7. $y = -\frac{3}{4}x + 3$

8. $y = \frac{2}{3}x - 3$

9. $y = -\frac{1}{2}x$

10. $(0,1)$ $(\frac{1}{3},0)$ $(1,-2)$ $(2,-5)$ Answers may vary.

11-14. Check student graphs.

15. $y = \frac{2}{3}x - 2$ Check student graph.

16. a. 6 **b.** 6

SKILLS PRACTICE 61

1. $(6,0)$ $(0,4)$

2. $(3,0)$ $(0,-4)$

3. $(1,0)$ $(0,-5)$

4. $(9,0)$ $(0,3)$

5. $(-5,0)$ $(0,5)$

6. $(6,0)$ $(0,9)$

7. $(-4,0)$ $(0,3)$

8. $(-\frac{2}{3},0)$ $(0,-2)$

9. a. $y = \frac{2}{3}x - 1$ **b.** $(0,-1)$ $(3,1)$ $(6,3)$ Answers may vary. **c.** Graph **d.** $(\frac{3}{2},0)$ $(0,-1)$ **e.** Graph **f. i.** $(\frac{3}{2},0)$ **ii.** $(0,-1)$

10. a. $(0,0)$ $(0,0)$ **b.** The x- and y-intercepts are the same point; two distinct points are required to establish a line.

11. $\{\frac{11}{2}\}$ **12.** $\{-\frac{1}{5}\}$ **13.** $\{9.5,-6.5\}$

14. $\{4,-1\}$ **15.** $\{3,2\}$

SKILLS PRACTICE 62

1. a. graph **b.** rise 2 run 5 **c.** $\frac{2}{5}$ **d.** $(8,6)$

2. a. graph **b.** rise -4 run 1 **c.** -4 **d.** $(-1,-9)$

3. a. graph **b.** rise 4 run 2 **c.** $\frac{4}{2}$ **d.** $(3,6)$

4. a. graph **b.** rise -3 run 6 **c.** $-\frac{3}{6}$ **d.** $(14,-5)$

5. a. $\frac{3}{2}$ **b.** $(0,4)$ **c.** graph

6. a. $-\frac{1}{2}$ **b.** $(0,5)$ **c.** graph

7. a. -1 **b.** $(0,3)$ **c.** graph

8. a. -4 **b.** $(0,-2)$ **c.** graph

9. a. 1 **b.** $(0,0)$ **c.** graph

10. a. 2 **b.** $(0,-6)$ **c.** graph

11. a. $y = -\frac{2}{3}x + 2$ **b.** $-\frac{2}{3}$; $(0,2)$ **c.** graph

12. a. $y = \frac{3}{4}x + 3$ **b.** $\frac{3}{4}$; $(0,3)$ **c.** graph

13. a. $y = x - 6$ **b.** 1; $(0,-6)$ **c.** graph

14. a. $y = -\frac{1}{2}x$ **b.** $-\frac{1}{2}$; $(0,0)$ **c.** graph

15. a. $(5,0)$ $(0,-3)$ **b.** $y = \frac{3}{5}x - 3$ **c.** $\frac{3}{5}$ **d.** graph

16. a. $(-8,0)$ $(0,-4)$ **b.** $y = -\frac{1}{2}x - 4$ **c.** $-\frac{1}{2}$ **d.** graph

17. a. $(-6,0)$ $(0,4)$ **b.** $y = \frac{2}{3}x + 4$ **c.** $\frac{2}{3}$ **d.** graph

18. a. $(5,0)$ $(0,-5)$ **b.** $y = x - 5$ **c.** 1 **d.** graph

19. $y = \frac{2}{3}x - 5$

20. $y = -4x + 3$

21. $(x - 2)(x - 1)$

22. $(x - 5)(x + 5)$

SKILLS PRACTICE 63

1. $(3,2)$ **2.** $(0,2)$ **3.** $(-1,-2)$

4. $(4,-1)$ **5.** $(-1,6)$ **6.** parallel

7. 2^5 **8.** transitive **9.** symmetric

10. assoc + **11.** comm ×

SKILLS PRACTICE 64

1. $\{(2,6)\}$ **2.** $\{(-4,-1)\}$ **3.** $\{(3,-1)\}$

4. $\{(-2,-7)\}$ **5.** $\{(3,0)\}$ **6.** $\{(-8,3)\}$

7. $\{(-2,-7)\}$ **8.** $\{(0,-2)\}$ **9.** $\{(8,4)\}$

10. $\{(\frac{1}{2},-1)\}$ 11. $(6,0), (0,-4), \frac{2}{3}$

12. $(6,0)$ $(0,-4)$ $(3,-2)$ Answers may vary.

13. $\frac{3}{4}$ 14. graph   15. $y = 4x - 5$

SKILLS PRACTICE 65

1. $\{(3,0)\}$ 2. $\{(8,4)\}$ 3. $\{(-4,-1)\}$

4. $\{(-2,-7)\}$ 5. $\{(0,-2)\}$ 6. $\{(-2,-7)\}$

7. $\{(-8,3)\}$ 8. $\{(0,2)\}$ 9. $\{(-2,\frac{1}{2})\}$

10. $\{(5,12)\}$ 11. $\{(-1,2)\}$ 12. $\{(3,4)\}$

13. $\{(5,0)\}$ 14. $\{(1,-6)\}$ 15. $\{(0.3,-1.2)\}$

16. $\{(\frac{1}{3},2\frac{1}{2})\}$ 17. a. 3 b. 13

18. a. -13 b. -13 19. $4x^2 - 12x + 9$

20. $4 - 3x$ 21. $2\frac{2}{3}$

SKILLS PRACTICE 66

1. a. up $r + e$; down $r - e$ b. $r = 3.5$ ft/s
   $e = 2.5$ ft/s c. about 4.09 mi/h d. 2.5 ft/s

2. graph $(0,-2)(3,0)$ 3. graph $(0,0)(2,2)$

4. graph $(0,5)(6\frac{2}{3},0)$ 5. $4x^3$ 6. 80

SKILLS PRACTICE 67

1. $\{(-1,1)\}$ 2. $\{(3,1)\}$ 3. $\{(-2,0)\}$

4. $\{(-3,-1)\}$ 5. $\{(0,3)\}$ 6. $x^2 + x + 6$

7. $2x^2 + x + 12$ 8. $\frac{4x}{3} - 2$

9. a. 2 b. $5\frac{1}{6}$ 10. a. 6 b. 36

SKILLS PRACTICE 68

1. Domain: $-4 < x \le 12$, range: $5 \le y < 9$

2. Domain: $-3 \le x \le 15$, range: $-2 \le y \le 6$

3. Domain: $-45 < x < 97$, range: $-56 < y < -24$

4–6. Check students' graphs. There are 2 graphs for each, one with positive slope and one with negative.

7. a. $y = 1.25x + 40$

   b. $56.25

   c. at most 16 loads

   d. Check students' graphs

8. a. $x =$ number of ounces, $y =$ dollar cost, $(20, 3.77)$ and $(14, 2.69)$

   b. 0.18

   c. $y - 3.77 = 0.18(x - 20)$ or $y - 2.69 = 0.18(x - 14)$

   d. solve for y; $y = 0.18x + 0.17$, fixed cost is 17¢

SKILLS PRACTICE 69

1. $x_{av} = 5.2$, $y_{av} = 5.2$, answers will vary for equation of line ($y = 0.791x + 1.089$)

2. $x_{av} = 0.3$, $y_{av} = -1.3$, answers will vary for equation of line ($y = -0.816x - 1.055$)

3. a. graph

   b. $x_{av} = 5.4$, $y_{av} = 1.1$

   c. answers will vary

   d. $y = 0.765x - 3.03$

4. a. graph

   b. $x_{av} = 9.35$, $y_{av} = 6.05$

   c. answers will vary

   d. $y = -0.529x + 10.99$

5. a. graph; yes

   b. $x_{av} = 4.1$, $y_{av} = 8.1$

   c. answers will vary ($y = 0.744x + 5.051$)

   d. ≈ 10

SKILLS PRACTICE 70

1. a. $\frac{5}{9}$ 2. a. $\frac{1}{13}$ 3. a. $\frac{1}{2}$

b. $\dfrac{2}{3}$

c. $\dfrac{1}{8}$

d. $\dfrac{4}{5}$

e. 1

b. $\dfrac{6}{13}$

c. 0

d. $\dfrac{6}{13}$

e. $\dfrac{6}{13}$

f. $\dfrac{5}{13}$

g. $\dfrac{7}{13}$

h. $\dfrac{5}{13}$

i. $\dfrac{3}{13}$

b. $\dfrac{5}{7}$

c. $\dfrac{5}{14}$

d. $\dfrac{2}{21}$

e. $\dfrac{1}{2}$

f. $\dfrac{16}{21}$

g. $\dfrac{1}{42}$

h. $\dfrac{2}{7}$

i. 0

GBGB
GGBB
GGGB
GBGG
GGBG
BGGG
GGGG

SKILLS PRACTICE 72

1. a. 35

b. 1.5

2. Check students' graphs. There are 2 graphs for each, one with positive slope and one with negtive.

3. Check students' graphs.

4. a. graph

b. $x_{av} = 17.15$, $y_{av} = 166.75$

c. answers will vary ($y = 10.97x - 21.35$)

d. $\approx$\$275

5. a. 30

b. 870

c. 24,360

e. $\dfrac{1}{24{,}360}$

SKILLS PRACTICE 71

1.a. $\dfrac{1}{13}$

b. $\dfrac{1}{26}$

c. $\dfrac{1}{2}$

d. $\dfrac{1}{52}$

e. $\dfrac{2}{13}$

f. $\dfrac{1}{26}$

g. $\dfrac{1}{52}$

h. $\dfrac{3}{26}$

i. $\dfrac{1}{13}$

2.a. (1,1), (1,2), (1,3), (1,4), (1,5), (1,6),

(2,1), (2,2), (2,3), (2,4), (2,5), (2,6),

(3,1), (3,2), (3,3), (3,4), (3,5), (3,6),

(4,1), (4,2), (4,3), (4,4), (4,5), (4,6),

(5,1), (5,2), (5,3), (5,4), (5,5), (5,6),

(6,1), (6,2), (6,3), (6,4), (6,5), (6,6)

b. 6

c. $\dfrac{1}{6}$

d. $\dfrac{1}{12}$

e. $\dfrac{5}{6}$

f. $\dfrac{3}{4}$

3.a. BBBG
BBGB
BGBB
GBBB
BBBB
BBGG
BGBG
GBBG
BGGB

b. $\dfrac{3}{8}$

c. $\dfrac{11}{16}$

d. $\dfrac{5}{16}$

e. $\dfrac{1}{4}$

SKILLS PRACTICE 73

1. 2, 3, 5, 7, 11, 13, 17, 19, 23, 29, 31, 37

2. $2 \cdot 3^2$

3. $2^3 \cdot 3$

4. $2^4 \cdot 3$

5. $3 \cdot 5^2$

6. $2^3 \cdot 3 \cdot 5$

7. $2^3 \cdot 5 \cdot 7$

8. $5^2 \cdot 13$

9. $2^2 \cdot 3 \cdot 11$

10. 5^4

11. 3^5

12. 7^3

13. $3^2 \cdot 5 \cdot 17$

14. $2^3 \cdot 5^3$

15. $3^2 \cdot 13 \cdot 17$

16. $3^2 \cdot 13^2$

17. $11 \cdot 19^2$

18. $2^3 \cdot 3^2 \cdot 5^3$

19. $2 \cdot 29 \cdot 37$

20. $2^7 \cdot 3^2 \cdot 5 \cdot 7$ **21.** 15 mi/h

22. 2:06 PM **23.** $14\frac{2}{3}$ **24.** $-2\frac{1}{12}$

25. $-\frac{10}{11}$

SKILLS PRACTICE 74

1. x^4y^2 **2.** $4x^3$ **3.** $8x^3$

4. x^4y^4 **5.** x^8 **6.** 16

7. -432 **8.** 128   **9.** 512

10. 32   **11.** 32   **12.** 64

13. 64   **14.** x^5 **15.** x^7

16. x^6 **17.** x^{10} **18.** x^2y^2

19. x^3y^6 **20.** $8x^3$ **21.** x^3y^6

22. $x^2 + 4xy + 4y^2$ **23.** $-3x^2 + 11x - 13$

24. $\frac{2}{3}x + \frac{4}{3}$ **25.** $\{(8,4)\}$ **26.** $\frac{3}{2}$

SKILLS PRACTICE 75

1. $(x^a)(x^b) = x^{a+b}$ **2.** $(x^a)^b = (x^{ab})$

3. $(xy)^a = x^ay^a$ **4.** x^5

5. x^7 **6.** x^6 **7.** x^{12}

8. $4x^5$ **9.** $12x^7$ **10.** x^7

11. $5x^5$ **12.** $10x^{11}$ **13.** $6x^7y^2$

14. $8x^3$ **15.** x^3y^3 **16.** x^3y^3

17. x^8y^{12} **18.** $-8x^6$ **19.** $27x^6$

20. $-10x^4$ **21.** $5x^{11}$ **22.** $256x^6$

23. x^8 **24.** x^{15} **25.** $243x^5$

26. $24x^6$ **27.** $-576x^3$ **28.** $x^3 + x^2$

29. $2x^2$ **30.** $4x^3$ **31. a.** undf **b.** 0

32. $\{-2\}$ **33.** {reals}   **34.** $\{5\}$

34. $\{-3, -1\}\}$

SKILLS PRACTICE 76

1. x^4 **2.** x^6 **3.** 16

4. -8 **5.** $6y^3$ **6.** $12x^3$

7. $2y$ **8.** $4x^3$ **9.** $-6x^2$

10. $9x^3$ **11.** $3x^3y^4$ **12.** $-4x^7$

13. x **14.** x^2y^2 **15.** $x^{11}y^4$

16. $\frac{y^7}{x^4}$ **17.** $\frac{1}{x^8}$ **18.** $\frac{4x^6}{9y^4}$

19. x^4y^9 **20.** x^5y^6 **21.** $3x^2$

22. $27x^6y^3$ **23.** $x^4 + x^5$ **24.** x^3y^2

25. $6x^8$

SKILLS PRACTICE 77

1. $\frac{1}{8}$ **2.** $\frac{1}{9}$ **3.** $\frac{1}{16}$

4. $-\frac{1}{125}$ **5.** $\frac{9}{4}$ **6.** 8

7. a. 5 **b.** $-\frac{1}{5}$ **c.** 1   **8.** x^{-3}

9. y^{-8} **10.** x^{-2} **11.** x^{-5}

12. x^4 **13.** $\frac{1}{8}x^{-3}$ **14.** x^7y^7

15. $2x^{-6}$ **16.** x^{-6} **17.** y^7

18. $x^{-2}y^{-1}$ **19.** $\frac{1}{9}x^{-1}$ **20.** $x^{-4}y^3$

21. $-\frac{1}{2}x^2y^{-2}$ **22.** $4x^6$ **23.** $6x^5$

24. $15x^3 - 12x^2$ **25.** $12x^2 + 5x - 2$

26. $-2x^2 + 10x - 9$

SKILLS PRACTICE 78

1. 2.13×10^2 **2.** 1.23×10^{-2}

3. 6.5×10^4 **4.** 9.08×10^{-3}

5. 5×10^{-2} **6.** 89,000

7. -0.00738 **8.** 4.5

9. 0.000024567   **10.** 1.23

11. 6×10^5 **12.** 9×10^1

13. 2×10^2 **14.** 4.2×10^{-6}

15. 4×10^6 **16.** 2×10^3

17. 8×10^{-3} **18.** 7.5×10^{-12}

19. 9.8325×10^{11} **20.** 9.2043×10^{-2}

21. 1.2105263×10^{-5}

22. 9.702259×10^{-4}

23. $9x^4$ 24. x^7 25. x^8y^{12}

26. $\frac{2}{3}x^7$ 27. $x + 6$

SKILLS PRACTICE 79

1. 3.7152×10^6 2. a. 2.0454×10^4

b. 8.766×10^3 c. 2.33 3. 3×10^{10}

4. $2.83824 \times 10^9 + 1.9008 \times 10^6$

5. 1.2×10^{32} calories

6. $5x^2$ 7. $6x^4$ 8. $81x^8y^{12}$

9. $9x^2y^{-2}$ 10. $x^2 + 4xy + 4y^2$

SKILLS PRACTICE 80

1. x^5 2. x^6 3. x^{-1}

4. $x^2 + x^3$ 5. $6x^7$ 6. $8x^3$

7. $x^{15}y^{-15}$ 8. $4x^2$ 9. $\frac{1}{9}$

10. $-18x^2$ 11. $8x^6y^9$ 12. $x^{12}y^{-8}$

13. $\frac{1}{4}x^6y^6$ 14. x^3 15. $8x^6$

16. $2x^3$ 17. $x^{10}y^{-20}$ 18. $-8x^{12}$

19. $x^{-8}y^6$ 20. 1 21. 3.0405×10^4

22. 9.1×10^{-4} 23. 9.2185×10^3

24. 0.0078 25. 7800 26. 8×10^1

27. 2×10^{-5}

SKILLS PRACTICE 81

1. $x^2 + 5x + 6$ 2. $2x^2 - 5x - 12$

3. $9x^2 - 1$ 4. $4x^2 + 20x + 25$

5. $6x^2 - 7x - 20$ 6. $(x - 3)(x - 2)$

7. $(x - 3)(x + 2)$ 8. $(x + 3)(x + 3)$

9. $(2x + 3)(x - 2)$ 10. $(2x + 3)(2x - 1)$

11. 4 12. 6 13. 12

14. 28 15. 18 16. x^2

17. x^2 18. $4x^3$ 19. $2x$

20. $6x^2y^5$ 21. x^2 22. $2x^5$

23. $4x$ 24. $4x^3y$

25. a. $y = 4x - 8$ b. 4 c. -8

26. $\{(4, -1)\}$ 27. -3

28. $(0,2)(3,0)(-6,6)$ Answers may vary.

29. $2x + 9$

SKILLS PRACTICE 82

1. $3(x + 1)^2$ 2. $5(x - 2)^2$

3. $6(x - 1)(x + 1)$ 4. $9(x - 3)(x + 3)$

5. $4(x - 4)(x + 3)$ 6. $2(2x + 1)(x + 2)$

7. $2(3x - 1)(x + 1)$ 8. $3(5x + 1)(x + 1)$

9. $2(x - 4)(x - 3)$ 10. $4(2x - 3)(x + 4)$

11. $6(2x + 1)(x + 3)$ 12. $3(2x - 3)(2x - 1)$

13. $5(x - 6)(x + 2)$ 14. $7(x + 3)(x + 3)$

15. $5(x - 10)(x + 5)$ 16. $8(x^2 + 1)$

17. $x(x - 8)(x + 8)$ 18. $x^2(x - 1)^2$

19. $5y^2(x - 4)(x - 3)$ 20. $x^2(x - y)(x + y)$

21. $27x^6$ 22. $5x^4$ 23. $2 + 8x$

24. $9x^2 - 6x + 1$ 25. $20x^9$

SKILLS PRACTICE 83

1. $(x + 2)(y + z)$ 2. $(x - 3)(x + 3)$

3. $(x + 8)(2x + 1)$ 4. $(y + 1)(y - 4)$

5. $(x + 1)(2x + 3)$ 6. $(x - 1)(4 - x)$

7. $(8x - 1)(5x - 1)$ 8. $2(2x - 1)(x - 2)$

9. $2(2x - 1)(5x - 6)$ 10. $(9x + 1)(9x + 2)$

11. $(x - 5)^2(x + 5)$ 12. $(3x + 1)(3x - 1)^2$

13. $(x - 2)(x + 2)(x - 4)$

14. $(x - 3)(x + 3)(x - 2)(x + 2)$

15. $(x - 3y)(x + 3y)(3x + 1)$

16. $(2x + 9)(x - 2)$ 17. $(3x + 4)(3x - 1)$

18. $(x - 3)(x - 2)$ 19. $(x - 2)(x - 3)^2$

20. $(x + 2)(x - 1)(2x + 1)$

21. $(x - 3)(x + 3), (x - 3)^2$; GCF $(x - 3)$

22. $(x - 1)(x + 1), (x - 1)^2$; GCF $(x - 1)$

138   *Answers*

23. $3(x + 3)$, $(x - 3)(x + 3)$; GCF $(x + 3)$

24. 36   **25.** 6   **26.** 12

27. 36   **28.** $58\frac{1}{3}$

SKILLS PRACTICE 84

1. $(x + b)(x + a)$ **2.** $(x + y)(x + 2)$

3. $(x + b)(2x + a)$ **4.** $(2x + b)(3x + a)$

5. $(x + y)(x - 3)$ **6.** $(3x + y)(2x - 3)$

7. $(3x - y)(2x - 1)$ **8.** $(x - z)(x - y)$

9. $(x - 5z)(2x - 1)$ **10.** $(x - 4y)(5x - 3)$

11. $(x - 2)(x + 2)(x + 3)$

12. $(x - 1)(x + 1)(2x + 3)$

13. $(x - 3)(x + 3)^2$

14. $(x^2 + 2)(x - 1)(x + 1)$

15. $(x^2 + 5)(x + 3)$

16. $(x - 1)(x + 1)(x - 2)$

17. $(x^2 + 1)(x - 2)$ **18.** $(6x + 7)(5x + 1)$

19. $(2x - 3)(4x + 1)$ **20.** $(3x - 4)(5x - 2)$

21. $\{11\}$ **22.** $\{11, -14\}$

23. $\{1, -4\}$ **24.** $\{1, -4\}$ **25.** $\varnothing$

SKILLS PRACTICE 85

1. $(5x + 3)(6x + 1)$ **2.** $(6x + 5)(4x + 3)$

3. $(3x - 4)(2x - 7)$ **4.** $(3x - 8)(2x - 5)$

5. $(3x - 2)(2x - 7)$ **6.** prime

7. $(3x + 5)(2x - 3)$ **8.** $(3x + 1)(2x - 5)$

9. $(3x - 2)(2x + 3)$ **10.** prime

11. $(3x + 1)(2x + 3)$ **12.** $(3x - 2)(2x + 5)$

13. $(2x + 5)(2x - 3)$ **14.** $(3x + 2)(2x - 7)$

15. $(5x + 3)(2x - 3)$ **16.** $2(2x - 5)(2x + 3)$

17. $4(3x - 5)(2x + 1)$ **18.** $3x^2(x - 3)^2$

19. $2x(3x + 1)(3x - 5)$

20. $25(x^2 + 1)$ **21.** $9(x - 3)(x + 3)$

22. $(x^2 + 1)(x - 6)$ **23.** $(x - 2)(x + 2)^2$

24. $(x - 1)(x + 1)(x + 3)$

25. $(x^2 + 1)(3x - 5)$

SKILLS PRACTICE 86

1. $\{-2, -2.5\}$ **2.** $\{1.5, -0.2\}$

3. $\{-\frac{1}{2}, 6\}$ **4.** $\{-\frac{1}{8}, \frac{3}{7}\}$

5. $\{2, -4, -5\}$ **6.** $\{-\frac{3}{2}, \frac{1}{4}, -\frac{3}{5}\}$

7. $\{3, 2\}$ **8.** $\{3, -2\}$

9. $\{\frac{1}{2}, 1\}$ **10.** $\{\frac{1}{2}, -\frac{1}{2}\}$

11. $\{\frac{3}{2}, 1\}$ **12.** $\{\frac{1}{3}, -\frac{3}{2}\}$

13. $\{4, 3\}$ **14.** $\{\frac{1}{2}, \frac{5}{2}\}$

15. $\{-1, 2\}$ **16.** $\{3, -3\}$

17. $\{\frac{-5 \pm 3\sqrt{5}}{2}\}$ **18.** $\{\pm 2\sqrt{2}\}$

19. $\{-\frac{3}{2}, -2\}$ **20.** $\{\frac{5}{3}, 1\}$

21. $8(x - 1)(x + 1)$ **22.** $4(x^2 + 1)$

23. $4(x + 1)^2$ **24.** $9(x - 3)(x + 3)$

25. $(x - 1)(x + 1)(3x + 4)$

SKILLS PRACTICE 87

1. $3(x - 1)(x + 3)$ **2.** $x^2(x - 2)(x + 1)$

3. $5(x - 5)(x + 5)$ **4.** $4(2x - 1)(x - 3)$

5. $(x - 5)(2x + 3)$ **6.** $(x + 2)(x - 2)^2$

7. $(8x - 1)(3x + 1)$

8. $(x + 2)(x + 1)(2x - 1)$

9. $(x^2 + 1)(2x + 3)$ **10.** $(x - 3)(x + 3)^2$

11. prime

12. $(x + 2)(x - 2)(x + 3)$

13. $(3x - 5)(2x + 3)$ **14.** $(5x - 1)(3x + 5)$

15. $(3x + 1)(3x - 2)$ **16.** $\{-4, -3\}$

17. $\{\frac{7 \pm \sqrt{97}}{2}\}$ **18.** $\{5, -4\}$

19. $\{-1, 4\}$ **20.** $x - 2$

SKILLS PRACTICE 88

1. a. $-\frac{4}{3}$ b. undefined c. $4\frac{1}{2}$

2. a. $-\frac{1}{4}$ b. -4 c. undefined

3. $\frac{3}{2}$ 4. $\frac{13}{12}$ 5. $\frac{5}{12}$ 6. $\frac{9}{16}$

7. $-\frac{43}{75}$ 8. $\frac{7}{30}$ 9. $\frac{5}{8}$ 10. $\frac{1}{50}$

11. -2 12. 1 13. $\frac{1}{8}$ 14. $\frac{7}{6}$

15. $\frac{3}{7}$ 16. 24 17. $2\frac{1}{9}$ 18. $\frac{1}{6}$

19. $\frac{5}{12}$ 20. $\{2,-1\}$ 21. $\{-1,4\}$

22. $\{3,2\}$ 23. $\{2,9\}$ 24. $\{-2\}$

SKILLS PRACTICE 89

1. a. Terms are added. Factors are multiplied.
   b. They are equivalent to 1.

2. $\frac{3x}{2y}$ 3. $2y$ 4. $3x$

5. $\frac{x+2}{2}$ 6. $\frac{4x-6}{x}$ 7. $\frac{8x^2-2xy}{y}$

8. $x-3$ 9. $x-2$ 10. $\frac{3x}{2}$

11. $\frac{x-2}{x}$ 12. $x-3$ 13. $\frac{2x+1}{2x}$

14. 4 15. $\frac{x+2}{x-2}$ 16. $\frac{x-1}{x-3}$

17. $\frac{x-3}{2x+12}$ 18. $\frac{x-3}{x+3}$

19. $\frac{x-2}{x+1}$ 20. x^2

21. 2 22. -4 23. $\frac{2}{5}$

24. There are no common factors.

25. x^2+1, x^2+3, etc.

SKILLS PRACTICE 90

1. $6y$ 2. x 3. $\frac{2}{x-4}$

4. $\frac{1}{2}$ 5. $\frac{x-5}{5x}$ 6. $\frac{2x-6}{3x+6}$

7. $\frac{9x-27}{x^2+3x}$ 8. $\frac{1}{2}$ 9. 12

10. $\frac{x}{5x-5}$ 11. $\frac{1}{3}$ 12. $\frac{1}{x}$

13. $\frac{x^2-2x+1}{4x}$ 14. $\frac{1}{3x+3}$

15. $\frac{x+3}{x-3}$ 16. $\frac{8}{y}$ 17. 2

18. $\frac{x+3}{9x+18}$ 19. $\frac{4x^2}{9y}$

20. $\frac{x-3}{2x}$ 21. $\frac{1}{6}$ 22. $\frac{3}{2}$

23. $-\frac{3}{8}$ 24. $-\frac{1}{12}$ 25. $\frac{49}{30}$

SKILLS PRACTICE 91

1. a. GCF $= 3x$ b. LCM $= 9x$

2. a. GCF $= 4$ b. LCM $= 24x$

3. a. GCF $= x^2$ b. LCM $= 15x^5$

4. a. GCF $= 1$ b. LCM $= 24x$

5. a. GCF $= 6$ b. LCM $= 6v\,(v-5)$

6. a. GCF $= r+5$ b. LCM $= r\,(r+5)$

7. a. GCF $= x-6$
   b. LCM $= (x-6)\,(x+5)\,(x+6)$

8. a. GCF $= x+7$
   b. LCM $= (x+7)\,(x+1)$

9. a. GCF $= x-5$
   b. LCM $= (x-2)\,(x-5)$

10. a. GCF $= 5$
    b. LCM $= 10\,(x-2)\,(x+2)\,(x-1)$

11. a. LCD $= x^3$
    b. $\frac{x^2}{x^3}$; $\frac{2x}{x^3}$; $\frac{3}{x^3}$
    c. $\frac{x^2+2x+3}{x^3}$

12. a. LCD $= 6x$ b. $\frac{10}{6x}$; $\frac{12}{6x}$ c. $\frac{11}{3x}$

13. a. LCD $= 24$ b. $\frac{3x}{24}$; $\frac{10x}{24}$ c. $\frac{13x}{24}$

14. **a.** LCD = $8xy$ **b.** $\dfrac{7}{8xy}, \dfrac{6y}{8xy}, \dfrac{8x}{8xy}$

 c. $\dfrac{7 + 6y - 8x}{8xy}$

15. **a.** LCD = 24 **b.** $\dfrac{3x}{24}; \dfrac{4x + 8}{24}$ **c.** $\dfrac{7x + 8}{24}$

16. **a.** LCD = 24 **b.** $\dfrac{3x}{24}; \dfrac{4x - 24}{24}$ **c.** $\dfrac{-x + 24}{24}$

17. **a.** LCD = $6y^2$ **b.** $\dfrac{4xy}{6y^2}; \dfrac{3 - xy}{6y^2}$

 c. $\dfrac{xy + 1}{2y^2}$

18. **a.** LCD = $12x^2$

 b. $\dfrac{10x}{12x^2}, \dfrac{16}{12x^2}, \dfrac{x^3}{12x^2}$ **c.** $\dfrac{10x + 16 - x^3}{12x^2}$

19. **a.** LCD = $18x$

 b. $\dfrac{30}{18x}, \dfrac{21}{18x}, \dfrac{2x^2}{18x}$ **c.** $\dfrac{9 + 2x^2}{18x}$

20. **a.** LCD = $10x^2$

 b. $\dfrac{3}{10x^2}, \dfrac{2x^2 - 6x}{10x^2}$ **c.** $\dfrac{-2x^2 + 6x + 3}{10x^2}$

21. $\dfrac{1}{12}$ **22.** $\dfrac{1}{18}$ **23.** $\dfrac{41}{20}$

24. $\dfrac{58}{21}$ **25.** 0

SKILLS PRACTICE 92

1. **a.** LCD = $x - 2$

 b. $\dfrac{4}{x - 2}; \dfrac{2}{x - 2}$ **c.** $\dfrac{6}{x - 2}$

2. **a.** LCD = $x - 3$

 b. $\dfrac{4x}{x - 3}; \dfrac{x + 4}{x - 3}$ **c.** $\dfrac{3x - 4}{x - 3}$

3. **a.** LCD = $2(x - 2)$

 b. $\dfrac{4}{2x - 4}; \dfrac{3}{2x - 4}$ **c.** $\dfrac{7}{2x - 4}$

4. **a.** LCD = $2(x - 2)$

 b. $\dfrac{4x}{2x - 4}, \dfrac{3x}{2x - 4}$ **c.** $\dfrac{x}{2x - 4}$

5. **a.** LCD = $4x^2$

 b. $\dfrac{5x^2}{4x^2}, \dfrac{12x}{4x^2}, \dfrac{8}{4x^2}$ **c.** $\dfrac{5x^2 - 12x + 8}{4x^2}$

6. **a.** LCD = $(x - 2)(x + 2)$

 b. $\dfrac{2}{x^2 - 4}, \dfrac{x^2 - x - 2}{x^2 - 4}$ **c.** $\dfrac{-x^2 + x + 4}{x^2 - 4}$

7. **a.** LCD = $24x$

 b. $\dfrac{15x^2}{24x}, \dfrac{72}{24x}, \dfrac{16}{24x}$ **c.** $\dfrac{15x^2 + 56}{24x}$

8. **a.** LCD = $(x - 2)(x + 3)$

 b. $\dfrac{x + 3}{(x - 2)(x + 3)}, \dfrac{x - 2}{(x - 2)(x + 3)}$

 c. $\dfrac{2x + 1}{x^2 + x - 6}$

9. **a.** LCD = $x - 3$

 b. $\dfrac{x^2}{x - 3}, \dfrac{9}{x - 3}$ **c.** $x + 3$

10. **a.** LCD = $(x + 2)(x - 3)$

 b. $\dfrac{x^2 + 2x}{(x - 3)(x + 2)}, \dfrac{5x - 15}{(x - 3)(x + 2)}$

 c. $\dfrac{x^2 - 3x + 15}{x^2 - x - 6}$

11. **a.** LCD = $(x + 4)(x + 2)$

 b. $\dfrac{2x + 4}{(x + 4)(x + 2)}, \dfrac{4x + 16}{(x + 4)(x + 2)}$

 c. $\dfrac{6x + 20}{x^2 + 6x + 8}$

12. **a.** LCD = $x(x + 1)$

 b. $\dfrac{x^2 + 2x + 1}{x(x + 1)}, \dfrac{x^2}{x(x + 1)}$

 c. $\dfrac{2x + 1}{x^2 + x}$

13. **a.** LCD = $20x^2$

 b. $\dfrac{12x}{20x^2}, \dfrac{120}{20x^2}, \dfrac{15x^2}{20x^2}$

 c. $\dfrac{15x^2 + 12x - 120}{20x^2}$

14. **a.** LCD = $(x - 2)(x + 3)$

 b. $\dfrac{7x + 21}{(x - 2)(x + 3)}, \dfrac{x^2 - 2x}{(x - 2)(x + 3)}$

 c. $\dfrac{x^2 + 5x + 21}{x^2 + x - 6}$

15. **a.** LCD = $2(x + 1)$

 b. $\dfrac{x^2}{2x + 2}, \dfrac{2x}{2x + 2}, \dfrac{1}{2x + 2}$

 c. $\dfrac{x + 1}{2}$

16. **a.** LCD = $6x(x - 2)$

 b. $\dfrac{5x - 10}{6x(x - 2)}, \dfrac{14x - 28}{6x(x - 2)}, \dfrac{4}{6x(x - 2)}$

 c. $\dfrac{-9x + 22}{6x^2 - 12x}$

17. **a.** LCD $= (x + 1)(x + 3)$

b. $\dfrac{8x + 8}{(x + 1)(x + 3)}, \dfrac{2}{x^2 + 4x + 3}$

c. $\dfrac{8x + 6}{x^2 + 4x + 3}$

18. **a.** LCD $= 3x(x - 3)$

b. $\dfrac{x^2}{3x(x - 3)}, \dfrac{9}{3x(x - 3)}$

c. $\dfrac{x + 3}{3x}$

19. **a.** LCD $= (x + 1)^2$

b. $\dfrac{x^2 + 2x - 3}{(x - 1)^2}, \dfrac{x}{(x - 1)^2}$

c. $\dfrac{x^2 + x - 3}{x^2 - 2x + 1}$

20. **a.** LCD $= 2x(x - 2)$

b. $\dfrac{x^2}{2x(x - 2)}, \dfrac{4}{2x(x - 2)}$

c. $\dfrac{x + 2}{2x}$

21. $4(x^2 + 1)$ **22.** $(3x - 5)(2x + 3)$

23. $(3x - 2)(3x + 1)$ **24.** $(2x + 3)(x^2 + 1)$

25. $(x + 3)^2(x - 3)$

SKILLS PRACTICE 93

1. $\dfrac{5y - x^2}{xy}$ **2.** $\dfrac{5}{y}$

3. $\dfrac{5y}{x^2}$ **4.** $\dfrac{x^2 + 4x + 8}{2x + 4}$

5. $\dfrac{x - 2}{2}$ **6.** $\dfrac{8}{x^2 - 4}$

7. $\dfrac{4x^2 + 5x}{x^2 - 2x - 3}$ **8.** $4x + 4$

9. $\dfrac{-x^2 + 3x - 7}{x^2 + x - 6}$ **10.** $\dfrac{x^2 - 5x - 4}{x^2 + x - 6}$

11. $\dfrac{4x^2 + 9x - 27}{3x^2 + 9x}$ **12.** 6

13. $\dfrac{4x}{x^2 - 25}$ **14.** $\dfrac{4x^2 - 3x - 1}{x^2 + 1}$

15. $\dfrac{12x + 36}{x - 3}$ **16.** $\dfrac{2x^2 + 4x}{x + 4}$

17. $\dfrac{x + 2}{2}$ **18.** $\dfrac{-4}{x^2 - 4}$

19. $\dfrac{3x^2 + 5x}{x^2 + 4x + 3}$ **20.** $\dfrac{2x + 2}{x + 3}$

21. $6x^5$ **22.** $2x^4$ **23.** $8x^3$

24. $14x^3 - 16x^2$ **25.** $\dfrac{x^3y^3}{8}$

SKILLS PRACTICE 94

1. $\dfrac{x + 3}{x - 3}$ **2.** -1 **3.** $\dfrac{x + 2}{2x + 1}$

4. $\dfrac{-3 - x}{x - 3}$ **5.** $\dfrac{x - 5}{2 - x}$ **6.** -4

7. $\dfrac{2}{x}$ **8.** $\dfrac{x}{3}$ **9.** $\dfrac{-3x - 9}{x - 3}$

10. $\dfrac{-3 - x}{x - 1}$ **11.** $\dfrac{6x + 4}{2x^2 + 3x + 1}$

12. $\dfrac{x + 1}{2x + 1}$ **13.** $\dfrac{2x^2 - 4x + 10}{x^2 - 2x - 3}$

14. $\dfrac{22 + x^2}{6x}$ **15.** $\dfrac{27 - x}{6}$ **16.** $\dfrac{-1}{x + 2}$

17. 4 **18.** $\dfrac{x}{2}$ **19.** $\dfrac{-x - 3}{9}$

20. $\dfrac{x - 18}{3}$ **21.** 4 **22.** 14

23. -4 or 14 **24.** $\emptyset$ **25.** $\{2,8\}$

SKILLS PRACTICE 95

1. $x + 4 + \dfrac{2}{x + 1}$ **2.** $x + 4 - \dfrac{3}{x + 2}$

3. $x + 6 + \dfrac{12}{x - 1}$ **4.** $x - 6 + \dfrac{20}{x + 3}$

5. $x + 3$ **6.** $x + 7 + \dfrac{23}{x - 4}$

7. $x - 2 - \dfrac{2}{x - 3}$ **8.** $x - 10 + \dfrac{47}{x + 4}$

9. $x + 9 + \dfrac{35}{x - 3}$ **10.** $x - 4 + \dfrac{9}{x + 1}$

11. $x - 5 - \dfrac{11}{x - 1}$ **12.** $x - 7 + \dfrac{17}{x + 2}$

13. $x + 12 + \dfrac{55}{x - 5}$ **14.** $x + 10 + \dfrac{36}{x - 4}$

15. $x + 6 - \dfrac{4}{x + 2}$ **16.** $x + 3 - \dfrac{3}{x + 3}$

17. $x + 1$ **18.** $x - 8 + \dfrac{2}{x - 1}$

19. $x - 1 + \dfrac{2}{x + 1}$ **20.** $x - 2 + \dfrac{8}{x + 2}$

21. $9x^2 - 12x + 4$ **22.** $9x^2 - 4$

23. $9x - 4$ **24.** $-9 - 9x$

25. $-x^2 - 12x - 64$

SKILLS PRACTICE 96

1. $x \neq -2$ **2.** $x \neq 3$ **3.** $x \neq 4$

4. $x \neq -3$ **5.** $x \neq 4, -1$ **6.** $x \neq -4, -3$

7. $10x$ **8.** $2x$ **9.** $2x(x + 2)$

10. $x^2 - 25$ **11.** $x^2 - 4x + 4$

12. $(x - 3)(x + 3)(x - 2)$

13. $x \neq 3$; LCM $= 3(x - 3)$; $x = 15$

14. $x \neq -5$; LCM $= 5(x + 5)$; $x = 5$

15. $x \neq -\dfrac{1}{2}$; LCM $= 5(2x + 1)$; $x = -3$

16. $x \neq -1$; LCM $= 3(x + 1)$; $x = -3$ or 2

17. $x \neq 0$; LCM $= 2x$; $x = 2$

18. $x \neq 0$; LCM $= 5x$; $x = 3$

19. $x \neq -1$ or 1; LCM $= x^2 - 1$; $x = 0.8$

20. $x \neq 2$ or -2; LCM $= (x - 2)(x + 2)$; $x = 3$

21. 6 **22.** -4 **23.** $m = \dfrac{2}{3}$

24. graph

SKILLS PRACTICE 97

1. $x = 3$ **2.** $x = 4.8$ **3.** $x = 3$

4. $x = 6.4$ **5.** $x = 15$ **6.** 87.5

7. $x = \pm 6$ **8.** $x = \pm 10$ **9.** $3:4$

10. $3:7$ **11.** $2:3$ **12.** $5:3$

13. 100 **14.** 169 **15.** 765

16. 40 **17.** 210 **18.** 75

19. commutative **20.** distributive

21. transitive **22.** reflexive

SKILLS PRACTICE 98

1. $\dfrac{p}{25}$ problems/min **2.** $\dfrac{x}{3}$ miles/min

3. $\dfrac{x}{5}$ situps/min **4.** $\dfrac{35}{x}$ dishes/min

5. 1 h 12 min **6.** $2\dfrac{2}{9}$ min

7. $666\dfrac{2}{3}$ s **8. a.** $\dfrac{1}{4}$ **b.** $\dfrac{1}{13}$ **c.** $\dfrac{1}{52}$

9. a. $\dfrac{13}{25}$ **b.** $\dfrac{12}{25}$ **c.** 0 **d.** 1

SKILLS PRACTICE 99

1. $\dfrac{43}{36}$ **2.** $\dfrac{1}{3}$ **3.** $\dfrac{10}{3x}$

4. $\dfrac{x^2 + 5x + 10}{x^2 + 2x}$ **5.** $\dfrac{2}{x + 2}$

6. 2 **7.** $\dfrac{2x - 1}{x^2 - 4}$ **8.** $\dfrac{x^2 - 6x - 7}{x + 3}$

9. $\dfrac{-x + 9}{x + 3}$ **10.** $\dfrac{4x + 2}{3x^2 + 6x}$ **11.** $\dfrac{x + 6}{x + 2}$

12. a. $-\dfrac{1}{2}$ **b.** 0 **c.** undefined

13. $x \neq 0, -2$; LCD $= x(x + 2)$; $x = 3$

14. $x \neq 0$; LCD $= 8x$; $x = -\dfrac{8}{3}$

15. $x \neq -4$; LCD $= x + 4$; $\emptyset$

16. $x = 6\dfrac{2}{3}$ **17.** 28 **18.** 255 **19.** 6 h per job

SKILLS PRACTICE 100

1. 1, 1; 4, 2; 9, 3; 16, 4; 25, 5; 36, 6; 49, 7; 64, 8; 81, 9; 100, 10; 121, 11; 144, 12

2. $2\sqrt{2}$ **3.** $3\sqrt{2}$ **4.** $2\sqrt{6}$

5. $3\sqrt{3}$ **6.** $4\sqrt{2}$ **7.** $2\sqrt{10}$

8. $3\sqrt{5}$ **9.** $4\sqrt{3}$ **10.** $9\sqrt{2}$

11. $5\sqrt{3}$ **12.** $8\sqrt{3}$ **13.** 15

14. $5\sqrt{2}$ **15.** $2\sqrt{15}$ **16.** $7\sqrt{2}$

17. $3\sqrt{10}$ **18.** $4\sqrt{6}$ **19.** $5\sqrt{6}$

20. $10\sqrt{2}$ **21.** $6\sqrt{15}$ **22.** $12\sqrt{10}$

23. 108 **24.** $30\sqrt{3}$ **25.** $192\sqrt{3}$

26. $3\sqrt{5}$ **27.** $-2\sqrt{3}$ **28.** $9\sqrt{6}$

29. $6\sqrt{5}$ **30.** $4\sqrt{2}$ **31.** $10\sqrt{2}$

32. $5\sqrt{3}$ **33.** $\sqrt{2}$ **34.** $-6\sqrt{6}$

35. $-7\sqrt{3} + 2\sqrt{6}$ **36.** $8x^2y^3(x-1)$

37. $x - 2$ **38.** $\dfrac{x+6}{3x^2}$ **39.** $\dfrac{x-2}{3x+9}$

SKILLS PRACTICE 101

1. $\dfrac{\sqrt{2}}{2}$ **2.** $\dfrac{3}{2}$ **3.** $\dfrac{\sqrt{15}}{3}$

4. $\dfrac{\sqrt{10}}{5}$ **5.** $\dfrac{\sqrt{10}}{5}$ **6.** $\dfrac{2\sqrt{10}}{5}$

7. $\dfrac{\sqrt{3}}{5}$ **8.** $\dfrac{\sqrt{10}}{10}$ **9.** $\dfrac{\sqrt{10}}{2}$

10. $\sqrt{5}$ **11.** $\dfrac{8\sqrt{5}}{5}$ **12.** $\dfrac{3\sqrt{2}}{2}$

13. $\dfrac{5\sqrt{14}}{14}$ **14.** $\dfrac{\sqrt{3}}{2}$ **15.** $\dfrac{\sqrt{15}}{9}$

16. $\dfrac{4}{9}$ **17.** $\dfrac{3}{2}$ **18.** $\dfrac{\sqrt{10}}{3}$

19. $\dfrac{5\sqrt{3}}{3}$ **20.** $\dfrac{\sqrt{10}}{3}$ **21.** $\dfrac{7x+24}{6x}$

22. $\dfrac{15}{16}$ **23.** $\dfrac{(x+2)(x^2+1)}{2x^6 + 2x^5}$

24. $9(x-3)(x+3)$

25. $(x-2)(x+2)(x+1)$

SKILLS PRACTICE 102

1. $\sqrt{3} + \sqrt{6}$ **2.** $\sqrt{6} + 2$

3. $5\sqrt{2} + 5\sqrt{3}$ **4.** $3\sqrt{2} + 2\sqrt{3}$

5. $3 + 2\sqrt{2}$ **6.** $3 - \sqrt{3}$

7. 1 **8.** 29

9. $5 + 2\sqrt{6}$ **10.** 1

11. $21 + 8\sqrt{5}$ **12.** $21 + 8\sqrt{5}$

13. $7 - 4\sqrt{3}$ **14.** $7 + 4\sqrt{3}$

15. $5 + 2\sqrt{6}$ **16.** $5 - 2\sqrt{6}$

17. $\dfrac{\sqrt{2}}{2}$ **18.** $\dfrac{\sqrt{6}}{2}$

19. $-3 - 2\sqrt{3}$ **20.** $-5 - 2\sqrt{6}$

21. $8\sqrt{5}$ **22.** $5\sqrt{5}$

23. $6\sqrt{2}$ **24.** $120\sqrt{2}$

25. $-5\sqrt{3} + 16\sqrt{2}$

SKILLS PRACTICE 103

1. $x = 31$ **2.** $x = 41$ **3.** $x = 12$

4. $x = 12$ **5.** $x = 1$ **6.** $x = 121$

7. $x = 8$ **8.** $x = 1$ **9.** $\varnothing$

10. $x = 8$ **11.** $x = 6$ **12.** $x = 12$

13. $x = 7.8$ **14.** $x = -7$ **15.** $\varnothing$

16. $x = 1$ **17.** $x = 9$ **18.** $x = 64$

19. $x = 2$ **20.** $x = -11$ **21.** $2\sqrt{7}$

22. $-4\sqrt{2}$ **23.** $15\sqrt{2}$ **24.** $\dfrac{\sqrt{30}}{4}$

25. $-\sqrt{2} - 2$

SKILLS PRACTICE 104

1. 5 **2.** 6 **3.** 3.61

4. 5.29 **5.** 1.41 **6.** 2.5

7. 13 **8.** 6 **9.** 5.66

10. 24 **11.** 7.14 **12.** 9.80

13. 9.75 **14.** 4.47 **15.** 9.95

16. 19.10 **17.** 3.61 **18.** 33.24

19. 3.46 **20.** 2 **21.** $11 + 6\sqrt{2}$

22. -7 **23.** $-\sqrt{2}$ **24.** $180\sqrt{2}$

25. 5

SKILLS PRACTICE 105

1. $5^{1/3}$ **2.** $16^{1/4}$ **3.** $12.3^{1/5}$

4. $8^{1/2}$ **5.** $128^{1/6}$ **6.** 1.71

7. 2 **8.** 1.65 **9.** 2.83

10. 2.24 **11.** 5 **12.** 3

13. 3 **14.** 9 **15.** 4.33

16. 8 **17.** 4 **18.** 2.83

19. 2.30 **20.** 2 **21.** $5\sqrt{2}$

22. $\dfrac{\sqrt{2}}{2}$ **23.** $2 + \sqrt{2}$ **24.** 11

25. $x = 4$

SKILLS PRACTICE 106

1. 0.375　　2. $2.\overline{6}$　　3. $0.41\overline{6}$

4. $0.\overline{7}$　　5. $1.\overline{285714}$

6. 0.3125　7. $0.1\overline{6}$　8. 2.4

9. $\frac{1}{3}$　　10. $\frac{2}{3}$　　11. $\frac{2}{9}$

12. $\frac{16}{99}$　　13. $\frac{8}{9}$　　14. $\frac{1}{99}$

15. irrational　　16. rational (2)

17. rational $(\frac{314}{100})$　　18. irrational

19. rational $(\frac{3}{10})$　　20. rational $(\frac{1}{3})$

21. $2\sqrt{2}$　22. 174　23. rational (2)

24. not real　25. $x = 5$

SKILLS PRACTICE 107

1. a. $2\sqrt{3}$, irrational b. 4, rational c. 45
   d. not real

2. $2\sqrt{6}$　3. $8\sqrt{2}$　4. $-5\sqrt{5}$

5. $8\sqrt{3}$　6. $2\sqrt{6}$　7. $48\sqrt{6}$

8. $5\sqrt{3}$　9. $\sqrt{3}(\sqrt{2}+1)$

10. $3 + 2\sqrt{2}$　11. -1　12. $2\sqrt{3}$

13. $\frac{\sqrt{6}}{4}$　　14. $2 - 2\sqrt{6} + \sqrt{3} - 3\sqrt{2}$

15. 5　　16. $12\sqrt{3}$　17. $-1 - \sqrt{3}$

18. a. $\frac{5}{9}$ b. $\frac{5}{99}$　　19. a. 5 b. 8.25

20. a. 9 b. 4.33 c. 3 d. 2.41 e. a and c

SKILLS PRACTICE 108

1-9.　Check student number lines.

10. $x > 3$　11. $x \leq -1$　12. $x \geq 5$

13. $x > -2$　14. $x \geq 4$　15. $x < 3.5$

16. $x \leq -1.3$ 17. $x \geq 6$　18. $x > -4$

19. $x < 0$　20. (0,–2)(3,0) graph

21. $-\frac{1}{4}$　　22. $\frac{3}{5}$

23. (4,0)(0,3)(2,1.5) Answers may vary.

SKILLS PRACTICE 109

1. $x > 3$　2. $x > -3$　3. $x \leq 17$

4. $x \geq 1$　5. $x \geq 3$　6. $x < 7$

7. $x \leq -4$　8. $x < -1\frac{1}{2}$　9. $x \geq -1$

10. $x \leq 5$　11. $x > 6$　12. $x \leq 3$

13. $x \geq 4$　14. $x < 4$　15. $x \geq 13$

16. $x \geq 0$　17. Ø　18. $x < -\frac{2}{3}$

19. $x \geq -22$　20. $x \geq -\frac{3}{5}$　21. {4}

22. {–7, 1}　23. {–3, 1}　24. {–14}

25. {1}

SKILLS PRACTICE 110

1-10.　Check student number lines.

11. $x < -3$ or $x > 5$　12. $1 \leq x < 6$

13. $-2 \leq x \leq 2$　　14. $x < -1$ or $x \geq 3$

15. $-4 \leq x \leq 2$　　16. $x < 2$ or $x > 12$

17. $2 \leq x \leq 12$　　18. $9 < x < 14$

19. $x < 0$ or $x > 6$　20. $2 \leq x \leq 4$

21. $-3 < x < 2$　　22. $-7 \leq x < -4$

23. $-15 \leq x \leq 4$　　24. absolute value

25. 3　　26. 21　　27. $x = 13, 5$

28. no solution　　29. $x = 9$

SKILLS PRACTICE 111

1. x is between 3 and –3.

2. x is not between –6 and 6.

3. $2x + 1$ is between –8 and 8, inclusive.

4. $2 - 3x$ is not between –8 and 8, inclusive.

5. $x + 5$ is not between –3 and 3.

6. $x - 6$ is between –5 and 5.

7. $|x| \geq 5$　　8. $|x + 2| \leq 6$

9. $|x - 5| \geq 7$　　10. $|2x - 3| \leq 8$

11. $-6 \leq x \leq 6$　　12. $x \leq -4$ or $x \geq 4$

13. $x < -9$ or $x > 3$　14. $2 < x < 8$

15. $x \leq -2$ or $x \geq 2$　16. $x < -4$ or $x > 4$

17. $-4 < x < 3$　　18. $x \leq -4$ or $x \geq 3$

19. Ø   **20.** all reals

21. No number can make 19 true or 20 false.

22. 20   **23.** 10, –20 **24.** 5

25. no solution   **26.** all reals, $x \neq -5$

SKILLS PRACTICE 112

1. $2x > 12$ **2.** $3x < 12$

3. $x - 5 \geq -8$ **4.** $x + 5 \leq 5$

5. $-3x \geq -15$ **6.** $-4x < 8$

7. $2x + 3 > 17$ **8.** $3x - 5 \leq -23$

9. $4x - 3 > -3$ **10.** $-2x + 5 \geq -21$

11. $4 - x \leq 2$ **12.** $2 - 3x \leq 5$

13. $3 < x + 5 < 9$ **14.** $4x + 3 \leq 27$

15. $100 - 6x \leq 100$ **16.** $45 + 3x \leq 345$

17. $4 < 2x + 4 < 14$ **18.** $9 \geq 3 - 2x \geq {}^{-}9$

19. 75 – 90

20. a. $30 - 2.50d$ **b.** 8 times

21. $x \geq -8$ **22.** $x > -3$

23. $-7 < x < 6$ **24.** $-14 \leq x \leq 2$

25. $x < -1$ or $x > 2$ **26.** Ø

SKILLS PRACTICE 113

1–20. Check student graphs.

21. $2^5 \cdot 3^2$ **22.** –20

23. $4x^2 - 4x + 1$ **24.** $9x^2 - 49$

25. $6x^2 - 20x + 8$

SKILLS PRACTICE 114

1. $x \leq -2$ **2.** $x > 2$ **3.** $x > -1$

4. $x \leq 2.3$ **5.** $x < -3$

6. $x < -2$ or $x > 2$

7. $-1 \leq x \leq 3$ **8.** $-3 < x \leq -1$

9. $x \leq -2$ or $x > 2$ **10.** $2 \leq x < 4$

11. $x \geq 1$ **12.** $x > -1$ **13.** $x \leq -4$

14. $-8 < x$ or < 6 **15.** $-2 < x < 4$

16. $x \leq -4$ or $x \geq 5$ **17.** $-\frac{1}{2} \leq x \leq 4$

18. $-2 < x < 5$ **19.** $x < -1$ or $x \geq 4$

20. $1 < x < -3$ **21.** $x \leq -4$ or $x \geq 4$

22. $-5 < x < 5$ **23.** $-4 \leq x \leq 3$

24. $1 < x < -2.5$ **25.** Ø

SKILLS PRACTICE 115

1. function   **2.** function

3. not a function   **4.** function

5. (–4,–1); (–3,0); (–2,1); (–1,–2); (0,3); (1,4); (2,5); (3,6); (4,7)

6. (–4,13); (–3,11); (–2,9); (–1,7); (0,5); (1,3); (2,1); (3,–1); (4,–3)

7. (–4,16); (–3,9); (–2,4); (–1,1); (0,0); (1,1); (2,4); (3,9); (4,16)

8. (–4,9); (–3,4); (–2,1); (–1,0); (0,1); (1,4); (2,9); (3,16); (4,25)

9. (–4,17); (–3,10); (–2,5); (–1,2); (0,1); (1,2); (2,5); (3,10); (4,17)

10. (–4,4); (–3,3); (–2,2); (–1,1); (0,0); (1,1); (2,2); (3,3); (4,4)

11.-15. Check student work.

SKILLS PRACTICE 116

1. direct, $k = 2$ **2.** inverse, $k = 18$

3. direct, $k = -\frac{8}{5}$ **4.** inverse, $k = -40$

5. $d = kh$ **6.** $t = ks$ **7.** $n = kt$

8. $n = kr$ **9.** $n = kh$ **10.** $d = kl$

11. $d = kn$ **12.** $l = \frac{24}{w}$ **13.** 7

14. 7 or –11 **15.** 1 or –5 **16.** 79

SKILLS PRACTICE 117

1. 0.87   **2.** 0.97   **3.** 1.11

4. $A = 60°$ **5.** $A = 38°$ **6.** $A = 45°$

7. 6.93   **8.** 11.49   **9.** 7.95

10. 19.53   **11.** 2.60   **12.** 6

13. 14   **14.** 34.85° **15.** 36.87°

16. 53.13° **17.** 48.19° **18.** 26.57°

19. 45°

SKILLS PRACTICE 118

1. –1, 4   **2.** –2, –3   **3.** 2, –1

4. –3, –4   **5.** 2   **6.** $-1, \frac{1}{2}$

7. 1, 5   8. none   9. –2

10. 12   11. 5   12. 2

13. (3, –4)   14. (–4, –20)

15. (1, 4)   16. (–2, –7)

17. (4, –7)   18. (–2, –6)

19. (1, 7)   20. (–5, –25)

21. $\dfrac{2x + 1}{x^2 - 1}$ 22. $\dfrac{x + 1}{x}$

23. $\dfrac{x - 1}{x^2 + 5x + 6}$ 24. $\dfrac{x^2 + 2x - 3}{x^3}$

25. $\dfrac{x + 3}{x + 2}$

SKILLS PRACTICE 119

1. $-7 \le x \le 1$ 2. $x < -1$ or $x > 9$

3. $x \le -2$ or $x \ge 1$ 4. $-2 < x < 3$

5. $-16 \le x \le 2$ 6. $x < -3\frac{2}{3}$ or $x > 1$

7. Ø   8. all reals   9. $x \le -7$ or $x \ge 3$

10. $-1 < x < 7$ 11. $1 \le x \le 7$

12. $x < -6$ or $x > 8$ 13. $x \le -8$ or $x \ge -2$

14. $-3 < x < 15$ 15. $x \le -7$ or $x \ge 1$

16. $-13 < x < -1$ 17. $x \le -2$ or $x \ge 4$

18. $-4 < x < 2$ 19. $2 \le x \le 4$

20. $x < -4$ or $x > -2$ 21. {1.14, –6.14}

22. {2, 3}   23. $4x^2 - 12x + 9$

24. $4\sqrt{3}$ 25. 53.13°

SKILLS PRACTICE 120

1. $-4 \ge x \ge -3$ 2. $-2 < x < 3$

3. $x \le -3$ or $x \ge 2$ 4. $-9 < x < 5$

5. $x \le -1$ or $x \ge 4$ 6. $x < 2$ or $x > 8$

7. $2 \le x \le 9$ 8. $-2 \le x \le 5$

9. all reals   10. Ø

11. $x < -0.36$ or $x > 0.56$

12. $-0.36 \le x \le 0.56$ 13. $-2.17 \le x \le 0.92$

14. $-1.45 \le x \le 3.45$ 15. Ø

16. a. –5 b. 5 and –1 c. (2, –9) d. graph

17. 10.63   18. $x - 3$

19. $18x^2y^3z$ 20. 109

SKILLS PRACTICE 121

1. a. i. –3 and 1 ii. –3 iii. (–1, –4)
   b. $x \le -3$ or $x \ge 1$ c. $-3 < x < 1$

2. a.–c. graph

3. 12.81   4. 53.13°   5. 56.31°

6. 6.13   7. 5.36   8. 4.24

9. a. $m = kg, k = 25$ b. 365 mi c. No. You
   can only travel for 32.5 miles more.

SKILLS PRACTICE 122

1. a. commutative multiplication
   b. associative addition c. symmetric
   d. distributive

2. a. $11 - 6x$ b. 53 c. $x = 3$ d. $x = 2$

3. a. $4x^2 - 4x + 1$ b. quadratic trinomial
   c. 49 d. $x = 3$ or $x = -2$

4. a. absolute b. 2; 14 c. 14 or –2; Ø
   d. $2 \le x \le 10$ e. $x > 11$ or $x < 1$

5. a. 35 b. $(2x - 1)(x - 2)$ c. $x = \frac{1}{2}$ or 2
   d. 2.28 or 0.22 e-f. graph

6. a. i. 4 ii. –8 b. 2 c. graph d. (5, 2)
   e. (3, –2) f. graph

7. a. i. $\frac{5}{3}$ ii. undefined b. $x = 1$ c. $x = -15$

8. a. $2\sqrt{3}$ b. $2\sqrt{2}$ c. No, cannot be written
   as a quotient of 2 integers. d. $x = 34$ e. $\dfrac{\sqrt{6}}{6}$